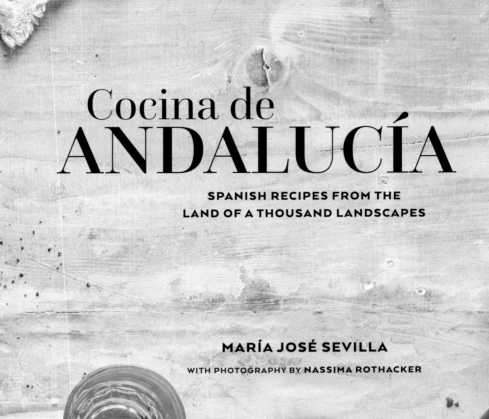

Cocina de
ANDALUCÍA

SPANISH RECIPES FROM THE
LAND OF A THOUSAND LANDSCAPES

MARÍA JOSÉ SEVILLA

WITH PHOTOGRAPHY BY **NASSIMA ROTHACKER**

RYLAND PETERS & SMALL
LONDON • NEW YORK

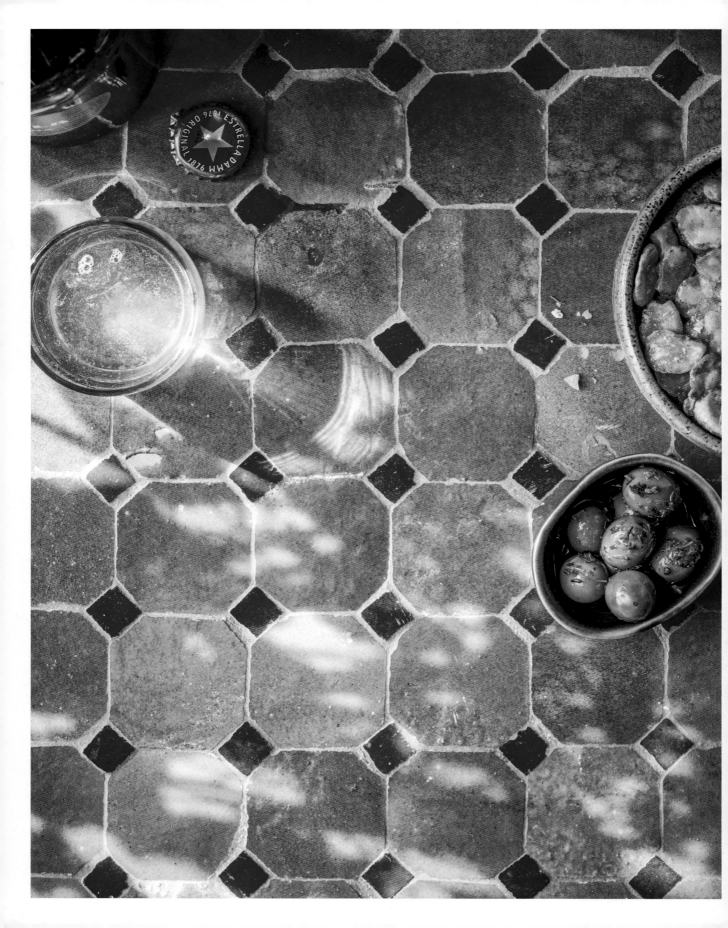

Contents

Introduction

Was it the light, the Andalucian light, the rich history of the place or the extensive vegetable garden that I fell in love with when I first visited El Zauzal. This small property at the heart of the Aracena National Park, 80 km northwest of Sevilla and just 60 km from the border with Portugal. The house was small and the track narrow, but the view lit by the light, which I cannot live without, awakens all senses any time of the day. It was in the middle of the summer, just in time to collect the flavoursome tomate rosa, the different coloured aubergines/eggplant, the green and the red (bell) peppers, the '*piel de sapo*' melon as well as the yellow courgettes/zucchini. There were also figs, plums and peach trees loaded with fruit, and others such as the pomegranate, quince and persimmon waiting for the arrival of the colder season. Eighteen years ago, we bought El Zauzal, a place capable of bringing happiness for doing either very little or very much, to cook delicious Andalucian food and to write books about the '*cocina de Andalucía*', this region that I have been travelling in for several decades while also working and living in London.

When I think of Andalucía, I do not think only in El Zauzal and the Sierras, I am equally attracted by the Mediterranean and the Atlantic coastal world, the small towns and beautiful cities dotted all along

the largest region of Spain. I also think of wheat fields, sunflower plantations, vineyards and olive groves, exuberant patios bursting with plants and balconies laden with colourful geraniums, all made especially beautiful with light, that special light that is an inspiration to me. Add to this scene, succulent prawns/shrimp from Huelva, fried fish wrapped in paper cones in Sevilla, fresh tuna from Cádiz, cold almond soup from Córdoba and Málaga, sweet things from Antequera, aubergines/eggplants with molasses from Granada, vegetable salads from Almería, also the amazing breads from Jaén and the varied and unique map of Andalucian food will begin to emerge.

To appreciate the complexity of the 'cocina de Andalucía' we need to go back in time to understand the importance of the legacy left by the different cultures who came and went, whose food has layered and is still present in the Andalucian cooking pot; Roman, Jewish and especially Moorish from North Africa and Middle East. Cocina Mozárabe (or Andalusi), is a term still used today to name dishes that were prepared by the Christian population living under Al-Andalus, the name given to Spain by the Moors. From the end of 15th century, the arrival of ingredients from the Americas enriched the Andalucian food culture, developed further by the imagination and creativity of modern chefs.

The climate has always played a key role in southern cooking. Moderate autumn/fall and winter temperatures, a beautiful springtime and a very hot summer have always dictated the mood of the Andalucian kitchen, totally dependent on the season and the locality, and joyfully resourceful, as are the people of the towns and villages of the region. A cold glass full of gazpacho Andaluz or salmorejo Córdobes, a plate of pan-fried wild red tuna served with an orange sauce, a salad of just-ripe tomatoes dressed with a local olive oil, a few drops of sherry vinegar and sprinkled with oregano, all dishes to taste while touring Andalucía.

In a land where the vine has been grown since the beginning of time, it is not difficult to find excellent wines to accompany food and to celebrate the many festive days present in the Andalucian calendar.

I cannot imagine a Spanish table full of tapas without a copita of fino or manzanilla sherry (fortified wines produced in the region of Cádiz in an area known as the 'sherry triangle'). This denomination of origin includes wines from Jerez de la Frontera, Sanlúcar de Barrameda and Puerto de Santa María. Montilla from a denomination known as Montilla-Moriles in Córdoba can be considered a cousin of sherry and is equally delicious, but it is mostly unfortified. Málaga wine is a sweet, fortified wine that is not only wonderful to drink with the desserts found in the region, but also used to give a layer of flavour to sauces served with meats and game. To complete the Andalucian wine picture there are quality white and also red wines now available on the market. Most recently I discovered the wines produced in the Denomination of Sierras de Málaga popularly known as 'the Ronda Wines'.

All About Ingredients in the Kitchens of Andalucía

Andalucía, with a good proportion of fertile land and the richness of the waters off its Atlantic and Mediterranean coasts, offers cooks great opportunities in the kitchen. To this has to be added the many different food cultures that for centuries have left behind agricultural and food legacies, unique and diverse, unmatched in the whole of the Iberian Peninsula. Which are the main ingredients associated with the Andalucian kitchen?

Out of the wide range of vegetables and fruits produced, I enjoy in particular the large chard which is available all year round as are the orange pumpkins which are excellent for preparing the *Flan de Calabaza y Caramelo* (Butternut Squash Caramel Flan) on page 176. In winter, oranges, both the bitter and the

sweet appear among the orange blossoms. At the start of spring tender broad/fava beans that can be eaten raw are collected from the numerous vegetable gardens dotted all over. With early summer come apricots, peaches and the very sweet dark cherries I adore. August is the month when the most delicious tomatoes and aubergines/eggplants are in season. Winter is the time to prepare quince paste and to enjoy pomegranate seeds as part of a dressing or as a dessert, sprinkled with a little sugar. At Christmas time, brightly coloured orange persimmons decorate their now leafless trees and some of the late olives, already of an intense black colour, are ready for picking to cure in salt.

Fish and shellfish dishes are plentiful. Preserved, fried, boiled, grilled, baked in salt, in soups and stews, salads or bathed with rich sauces, fish has simply been a favourite in the whole of Andalucía since ancient times. In the winter, members of the bream family are prepared in the oven over beds of potatoes covered with rich pepper sauces. In April the arrival of the wild red tuna is celebrated everywhere, especially in Cádiz where it is caught using an ancient fishing system known a '*Almadraba*'. Hake is beautifully fried as is the anchovy, the red mullet or the popular '*acería*' (wedge sole). The passion of the Andalucians for prawns/shrimp is also impressive. Some have a good size such as the red *carabineros* or the exquisite *Langostinos de Sanlúcar de Barrameda*. Also loved are the tiny, almost translucent '*camarones*' used in the preparation of the famous *Tortillitas* (see page 18) or the very tasty *coloarillos* fished in the waters off Málaga for example, but there are so many others.

All types of fresh meat are available everywhere but there are areas where some of the meats are preferred, especially fresh pork. You can also find a great selection of cured meats and sausages to eat

as they come, or to be included in many of the substantial dishes cooked in the region such as the *cocidos* y *potajes* (stews and hearty soups) or in a *bocadillo*, the Spanish answer to the filled baguette.

The Ibérico pig thrives in the forests of Salamanca, Extremadura and Andalucía and especially in the Sierra de Aracena in Huelva where we live. Today the survival of this animal, with dark skin and fatted belly who loves acorns, is a great success both from an ecological and commercial point of view. Nothing is wasted with the Ibérico, from the expensive cured hams and shoulders to the chorizos and black puddings. Furthermore, fresh ibérico cuts such as *pluma*, *secreto* or *solomillo* are now demanded by markets and restaurants in many places around the world.

A trip across southern Spain will give an idea of the importance of the olive and of olive oil. There are thousands and thousands of trees which appear in front of our eyes when travelling through. It is easy to find Andalucían olives packed in jars or cans in supermarkets and specialist shops, but is worth searching for some particular varieties such as the *Manzanilla de Sevilla* or the large green *Gordal*. You can eat them as they come just simply cured, or marinate them at home following traditional or modern recipes. Olives cannot be eaten raw but must be cured of their natural bitterness before they are edible. To me the most delicious olives are those which are freshly picked and cured within a few weeks. To cure raw olives they are crushed first with a mallet or slashed in a few places then soaked in water for one or two weeks, changing the water every day, after which they can be marinated following local recipes.

Andalucía is the largest olive oil producer in Spain and Spain is the largest producer in the world. Ancient Rome imported thousands and thousands of litres of olive oil from the region every year, as the quality and quantity of Andalucian olive oil surpassed that of their own production. It will be impossible to understand Andalucian food without the presence of olive oil in all types of recipes, including the extensive range of confections and sweet things cooked at home and in *pastelerías* (cake shops). Frying in olive oil is an art Andalucians mastered and its presence in dressings, marinades and sauces is becoming more and more relevant in traditional and modern dishes.

Sherry vinegar, no longer kept as the family secret in sherry *bodegas* has become an ingredient we all use these days in salads and stews, in marinades and even in some desserts.

Spices have a long history, especially in Andalucía. They were brought first by Phoenician traders to the ports they established all along the Andalucian coast. The Romans brought to all of their provinces, including Hispania, rich cargos from India. For many years, trade between East and West flourished in Europe until it was halted by the Arab conquest of Alexandria in the 7th century. Spain, in the hands of the Arabs until the 15th century, was the only part of Europe which still had access to spices. Today it is in Andalucían food where the presence of spices is most evident: cinnamon, saffron, sesame, aniseed, ginger, pepper and nutmeg among others. Fresh herbs are also equally important in Andalucian food.

Andalucians also love rice dishes. Rice was brought to the Iberian Peninsula by the Arabs in the 9th century. It was planted in many places including the delta of the Guadalquivir river. In this book I have added a number of traditional Andalucian recipes cooked with rice such as *Arroz con Pollo* (see page 134) which is prepared with sherry.

Pasta is another of the food gifts brought by the Arabs to Al-Andalus which has always been very appreciated in Southern Spain, especially *fideos*. The popular *Sopa de Picadillo* is prepared with chicken broth, rice or the thinnest fideos as well as boiled/cooked eggs, ham and mint. In Andalucía thick *fideos* are added to substantial fishermans' stews.

TAPAS &
RACIONES

The World of Tapas

In Andalucía, as elsewhere in Spain, exciting changes have been made to traditional Spanish food, but at the same time you can still find very many tapas bars everywhere that serve quality traditional food cooked to a really high standard, in which little has changed, including the excellent quality of the ingredients used.

In the last decades the perception of Spanish food outside the country has radically changed. It has moved from something relatively little known and treated with indifference to being seen as probably one of the best in the world. Several reasons have contributed to this, including the opening of top-quality Spanish restaurants and tapas bars around the world. These are now in the hands of professional Spanish chefs, backed up with suitable investment.

But what are tapas? Where did they come from? Who was initially responsible for the creation of such tantalizing food? Well, tapas are collections of small dishes. The word comes from 'tapar', to cover. Originally a 'tapa' was offered by a bartender for free, to customers drinking at the bar, so a *copita* (glass) of sherry would be covered with a small dish of something delicious, i.e. a 'tapa'. This custom still exists but it is slowly dying out. '*Tapear*' is to enjoy tapas in a bar with a glass of wine or a beer or in several different bars, perhaps in the same street, by yourself or with friends. Sometimes one or both will be eaten before lunch, or before dinner at night. A large portion of a '*tapa*' is known as a '*ración*'.

Today tapas have become more complex and a little more expensive. They are recognized now everywhere, but the real story started not so long ago in a very simple way. Tapas were born in Andalucía, and, to be precise, in Triana, a popular area of Sevilla on the west bank of the historic Guadalquivir river. Since the 19th century, numerous bars and restaurants here have been bringing pleasure to locals and visitors alike in a celebration of the way in which they prefer to eat and also to relate to other people.

Andalucía is a place where socializing matters: socializing with the bartender, with new faces you have only just met or socializing with family and friends around plates of delicious food. Here the real world of tapas exists more than in any other place – a perfect harmony between food, drink and above all people. Andalucians love informality and without doubt this is an informal way of eating.

Tapas can be very simple: a plate of marinated

olives, roasted almonds or *papas aliñás*, which is one of my favourites. *Aliñás* (see page 31) are potatoes served warm, flavoured with chopped red onion and parsley, dressed cleverly with extra virgin olive oil, vinegar and salt. Tapas offers samples of the extensive traditional recipes prepared at home or in the kitchens of local bars where excellent cooks, mostly women, have always been responsible for the food. Not so long ago we could never see them as they were always working behind the scenes. Nowadays they often come out to the 'front of house' in their chef's whites to greet their customers and recommend the dish of the day, whether that is artichokes in a 'blonde' sauce or *a la plancha* (from the grill) served with vinagrette or *salsa mahonesa* (mayonnaise), *pescaíto frito* (fried fish), which Andalucians know how to cook to perfection, or in spring, perhaps a complex rice dish prepared with mushrooms from the Sierras or seafood from the coast. The diversity of the tapas and their presence in different food scenarios is also part of

their success. As well as in local bars they are also offered in restaurants as small sharing plates at the beginning of the meal: a plate of Ibérico ham or *lomo* (cured pork loin), *langostinos* (tiger prawns/shrimp) from Sanlúcar de Barrameda, a ración of the house *Ensaladilla Rusa* (see page 109), some *chipirones* 'a la plancha' (grilled baby squid), a plate of *Pimientos de Padrón* (see page 31) or a salad of the best tomatoes to be found, dressed with a fresh olive oil from a local producer and sprinkled with salt flakes and oregano.

Another important factor now is the emergence of modern tapas created by innovative Spanish chefs in Spain and beyond, as well as the way these dishes have been incorporated into what was before a traditionally structured menu with a section of tapas at the very beginning. What intrigues me is how difficult it can be to identify them when a modern chef has altered a classic *tapa* by innovation, creating something even more delicious. They may appear in a menu as an appetizer or even as a main course with a longer or different name. Is a delicious red tuna tartar on a small square of toasted bread a *tapa* or an appetizer? Is a succulent and tender octopus leg perfectly grilled, served with the most delicious cream of potatoes and a fashionable *Mojo Rojo* a *ración* or a main plate? The price may not necessarily be an indication of the place a particular dish should be eaten during a meal, nor is the order in which dishes come out from the kitchen, but it cannot be over-stressed, it is the quality of the ingredients and the talent of the cook that make the difference.

Croquetas de jamón, huevo y pollo
HAM, EGG & CHICKEN CROQUETTES

Croquetas began as a way of combining leftovers with a béchamel sauce, to then be cleverly converted into another meal. The secret resides in a béchamel full of flavour. It is not surprising I am still making mine the same way as my mother and my grandmother did; they were wonderful. My own son Daniel makes amazing *croquetas de gambas* (prawn croquettes) and my granddaughter Sophie Maria's béchamel sauce is so delicious that my mother would have been very proud of her.

2 tablespoons Spanish olive oil, plus extra for greasing
½ a white onion, chopped
250 g/9 oz. chicken breast
2 tablespoons fino sherry or 3 tablespoons white wine
2 boiled (cooked) eggs, grated
50 g/1¾ oz. Serrano ham, chopped

FOR THE BÉCHAMEL
60 ml/¼ cup chicken stock (optional)
1 litre/4 cups whole/full-fat milk
75 g/⅓ cup butter or light olive oil
100 g/¾ cup plain/all-purpose flour
sea salt, to season

COATING
2 eggs
250 g/3 cups fine breadcrumbs
sunflower oil, for frying*

MAKES 24 CROQUETAS

In Andalucía practically all the food is fried in olive oil, but in the case of the croquetas I prefer to use sunflower oil.

Heat the olive oil in a frying pan/skillet and sauté the onion until soft. Add the chicken breast and sauté for a few minutes. Pour in the sherry or wine and cook until the liquid evaporates and the chicken has taken some colour all over. Set aside to cool. When cold, finely chop the chicken as if you were chopping parsley, then set aside.

To make the béchamel, first gently heat the stock and milk in a saucepan. In another saucepan melt the butter over a medium heat. Start adding the flour, little by little, until it becomes fully integrated with the melted butter (I use a wooden spoon). Start adding the warm milk and stock, little by little. To work the béchamel, change the spoon for a hand whisk, stirring almost continuously, until the taste of flour has disappeared completely and you have a smooth sauce – it will take at least 30–40 minutes.

Add the grated eggs, ham and chicken to the sauce and stir for a few minutes before checking and adjusting the seasoning. When ready, the béchamel should be creamy and very shiny with a light texture, but never too thin. It should be cold before frying, so pour the sauce onto a large plate, cover with clingfilm/plastic wrap and transfer to the fridge to chill.

In a bowl, beat the eggs very well (this is important) and place plenty of fine breadcrumbs in two large dishes.

To stop the soft béchamel getting stuck on your fingers, grease your hands first with olive oil. Take a small portion of the béchamel with your fingers or with a spoon and lightly shape into a ball. Place it in the first dish of breadcrumbs. Now it will be easier to shape the croquetas properly. Using a spoon, coat each croqueta in the beaten egg and then again in the breadcrumbs. Shape with your hands for the final time and repeat until all the béchamel has been used.

Heat the oil in a large frying pan/skillet or electric deep fat fryer to about 180°C/350°F. It is vital that this temperature is maintained to avoid the delicate croquetas splitting while they fry. Cook until crisp and golden. Serve the croquetas hot.

Tortilla de patata y mermelada de cebolla
POTATO OMELETTE WITH CARAMELIZED ONIONS

Spanish food is mostly regional, but the *tortilla* is one of the few national dishes. In Andalucía, you find tortilla offered as a 'tapa' in most bars and restaurants, or served as a light meal at home with a simple salad. Often it is filled with chorizo or peppers, but for me the best tortilla has only egg, potato and onions.

There is no traditional way of cutting the potato. It can be sliced thinly, as I do, sliced thickly or even diced. The potato should not be par-boiled but gently braised in plenty of olive oil with the onions, but the final result should not be greasy.

300 ml/1¼ cups Spanish olive oil (see Note on page 31)
2 white onions, thinly sliced
1 kg/2¼ lb. potatoes (Desiree or Maris Piper are both good)
6 medium/US large eggs
sea salt, to season

SERVES 6

First caramelize the onions. In a small saucepan heat a couple of tablespoons of olive oil. Add the onions and cook slowly until very soft, stirring frequently. Carry on cooking until they become brown in colour and very sweet. Reserve.

Before you start cooking the potatoes, select a frying pan/skillet light enough for you to lift with one hand and a plate light and big enough to cover the pan when it comes to turning the tortilla over. Place the plate near the sink.

Peel and slice the potatoes thinly. Rinse, pat dry and season with salt. In the pan, gently heat the remaining oil over a medium heat until a small piece of potato sizzles when dropped in. Now add all the potato and start cooking. You don't want the potato to take colour too fast, so gently turn with a fork or wooden spoon. Once the potatoes are nearly ready, add the onions. When the oil starts coming to the surface and the potato and onion are integrated and taking colour, tip all of it into a colander over a bowl to drain. Adjust the seasoning with salt if needed. Now beat the eggs in a large bowl and add the potatoes and onions from the colander, mixing thoroughly with a fork.

Pour 1–2 tablespoons of the reserved oil into the frying pan to thinly cover the base. When hot, pour the egg and potato mix and onion into the pan and cook for 2–3 minutes. Next gently push the tortilla away from one side of the pan to check that the underside is just light brown in colour.

Over the sink, place the plate on top of the pan and holding the plate firmly with the flat of your hand, rapidly invert pan and plate together with care so that the tortilla lands on the plate. Turn the pan right-side up and slide the tortilla back into the pan to cook the other side. Cook for another couple of minutes. Check the centre, which should remain fairly moist, with a wooden skewer. Place a clean plate on top of the pan so you can turn the tortilla back over again. Serve warm or cold, as preferred.

Huevos fritos de Codorniz con jamón Ibérico
FRIED QUAIL EGG & IBÉRICO HAM ON MINI TOASTS

This is a very popular tapas that is easy to prepare at home. The bread rounds can be fried or toasted as preferred, and the combination of a crispy fried quail egg and the Ibérico ham is pretty wonderful. *(Pictured on page 24.)*

olive oil, for frying
12 quail eggs
12 small round slices of bread
6 slices of Ibérico ham, cut into small
   pieces

cocktail sticks/toothpicks

SERVES 6 (2 EGGS PER PERSON)

Heat two fingers of olive oil in a small frying pan/skillet. When the oil is hot but never smoky, fry the quail eggs to a crispy texture. This will take no time. Set aside.

Maintain the temperature of the oil and start frying the small rounds of bread on both sides; reserve on kitchen paper.

Place each egg on top of a small round of fried bread then cover with the ham. Use a cocktail stick/toothpick to secure the bread, egg and ham to serve.

Choricitos al oloroso
CHORIZO IN OLOROSO SHERRY

People love chorizo and this is a recipe I serve when offering tapas at home. It is prepared with cooking chorizo that comes in different shapes and sizes. Some cooking chorizos are sausage shaped and others are small round balls known as '*choricitos*'. I make this as a *montadito*, which is something small and delicious mounted on top of a small piece of bread which I skewer with a little wooden stick.

The recipe can be made by cutting chorizo into slices or using the small round ones you can buy in butchers' shops in Andalucía. Today chorizo can be bought almost everywhere. These are also delicious made with cider in place of the Oloroso sherry.

250 g/9 oz. choricitos
   (or a ring of chorizo cut into slices)
300 ml/1¼ cups Oloroso sherry
rustic bread, to serve

SERVES 6

Place the choricitos in a frying pan/skillet and pour in the sherry. Bring to the boil and then reduce the heat. Simmer, uncovered, for 15 minutes.

Remove the pan from the heat and leave the choricitos to marinate for at least for 30 minutes.

Serve at room temperature on top of pieces of bread with some of the marinade spooned on top.

Chupito de remolacha y fresas
BEETROOT & STRAWBERRY SHOTS

In Spanish, a '*chupito*' is a small complimentary glass of liqueur or a digestif offered to restaurant diners after a meal. At home it is also the name we give to any refreshing fruit and vegetable drink served in a small glass as an alternative to Gazpacho Andaluz (see page 64). (*Pictured on page 25.*)

2 beetroot/beet, peeled and quartered
   (see Note)
250 g/9 oz. strawberries
   (or any other soft summer fruit)
250 g/9 oz. ripe tomatoes, peeled
250 g/9 oz. cherry tomatoes
1 garlic clove, sliced
100 g/3½ oz. cucumber, peeled
1 green (bell) pepper, deseeded and
   chopped
4 tablespoons Spanish extra virgin olive
   oil (not too strong in flavour)
sherry vinegar, to taste
sea salt, to season

SERVES 6

Juice the beetroot/beet in an electric juicer and set the juice aside.

Use an electric blender to blend the strawberries, tomatoes, garlic, cucumber and green (bell) pepper. Once blended, add the beetroot juice, then start adding the olive oil, slowly, followed by the vinegar.

Now taste it, in case some adjustment is needed and add more oil or vinegar as necessary, then season with sea salt. Place in the fridge until ready to serve in small shot glasses.

NOTE *Although the beetroot/beet juice can be obtained from both cooked or uncooked beetroot, my preference is from cooked.*

Aceitunas aliñadas
MARINATED GREEN OLIVES

In Andalucía, where the olive has always taken centre stage at the table, marinating them at the beginning of winter was a job home cooks felt proud to do and they tended to follow their own family's particular recipe. Today cured olives are easy to find in every local market, marinated in varying ways with many different aromatics; sometimes vinegar is added, but they are always tasty and very moreish. To make things easy for you here, I have used a jar of the Manzanilla olives so typical of the city of Sevilla.

2 medium oranges
3 tablespoons Spanish extra virgin
   olive oil
1 teaspoon sherry vinegar
2 teaspoons white sesame seeds
1 teaspoon freshly crushed black
   peppercorns
400 g/14 oz. manzanilla olives in a jar,
   drained and rinsed
a few small fresh mint leaves, washed
   and patted dry

MAKES ABOUT 400 G/14 OZ.

Wash the oranges and grate and juice one of them. Set the other aside.

In a bowl, using a hand whisk, mix the orange juice and zest with the olive oil and the vinegar.

Peel the second orange, removing all the pith and use a small knife to cut it into segments.

In a small frying pan/skillet, toast the sesame seeds until they take on a little colour and release their nutty aroma.

In a serving bowl, mix the toasted sesame seeds, peppercorns, olives, orange segments and mint leaves before adding the flavoursome juice. Blend well. These will keep in the fridge for several days.

Berenjenas con miel de caña
FRIED AUBERGINES WITH MOLASSES

After more than twenty years, I decided to visit Granada again. If I was to write a book about Andalucian food I needed to submerge myself in cities, towns and villages where I could find culture and a unique relationship with food. In Granada it has always been easy to do so. The city has seriously expanded, but the Alhambra is still as it was when built centuries ago: magnificent and unforgettable. In terms of food, Granada, a truly cosmopolitan city, is responding to the demand of a new generation of Spaniards as well as thousands of foreign students and other visitors. All are looking for modern Spanish food as well as dishes heavily influenced by for example Asia, but the informal way of eating loved by all Spaniards has not changed, nor have some of the dishes associated with traditional food, I am glad to say. In one of the smallest bars in town, Casa Juanito, I found a recipe I needed to include in the book. First the bartender brought me 'una caña' (a glass of very cold draft beer) and a gift from the kitchen: fried pieces of hake cooked beautifully by a woman chef in impeccable whites. Then it came the recipe I asked for, *Berenjenas con Miel de Caña* which were so crunchy and so utterly delicious.

1 large aubergine/eggplant, cut into very thin slices
sparkling water, for soaking
flour for frying (Spanish *harina semolosa de trigo**) or plain/all-purpose flour, for coating
Spanish olive oil, for frying
2 tablespoons molasses
sea salt, to season

SERVES 2

Harina semolosa de trigo is a special frying flour made from 100% Andalucían wheat flour. This flour is the authentic flour used to fry calamares and make proper pescadito frito.

Steep the sliced aubergine/eggplant in bowl of sparkling water with a little salt for about 10–15 minutes. Remove from the water and pat dry with kitchen paper.

Heat plenty of olive oil in a large frying pan/skillet (or even better, in an electric deep fat fryer). Coat the aubergine slices with flour and fry them in the hot oil, just enough to take colour. Pat dry gently.

Serve piping hot, lightly drizzled with the molasses.

NOTE *When vegetables and potatoes are fried in olive oil, the oil can be used again. Once cold, filter the oil through a sieve/strainer and keep it in a container. It retains a lovely flavour.*

Tortillitas de camarones de Cádiz
SHRIMP FRITTERS FROM CÁDIZ

These are not small omelettes/omelets as their name would suggest, but a thin cracker-like salty confection made traditionally by frying minute shrimps known as 'camarones' with shell and all, in batter. These *tortillitas* are a tantalizing speciality from Cádiz and the sherry production areas; Jerez de la Frontera, Puerto de Santa María and Sanlúcar de Barrameda. As it is not easy to find them fresh outside Andalucía, you may find them in a very specialized fishmonger. For this reason I have prepared these with fresh prawns/shrimp.

As it won't keep, the batter must be made at the last moment just before frying. Modern versions of the recipe are now including a seaweed known as 'sea lettuce', introduced for the first time by Fernando Córdoba in his restaurant El Faro del Puerto, in Puerto de Santa Maria.

40 g/¼ cup strong flour
40 g/¼ cup plain/all-purpose flour
250 ml/1 cup very cold water
1 large spring onion/scallion (cebolleta), white part only, chopped
2 tablespoons freshly chopped parsley or sea lettuce, fresh or hydrated
100 g/3½ oz. raw prawns/shrimp, heads removed, peeled and chopped into small pieces
Spanish light olive oil or sunflower oil, for frying
sea salt flakes, to serve

SERVES 4–6 DEPENDING ON SIZE

To prepare a batter, blend both the flours with the water using a hand whisk. Remember the water must be very cold. Add the spring onions/scallions and the parsley or sea lettuce, mixing continually. The texture should be similar to the texture of a fruit yogurt. Stir in the chopped prawns/shrimp.

Traditionally the tortillitas are fried in a paella pan with plenty of oil, but any similar flat frying pan/skillet will do the job. Heat the pan before pouring in the oil, about two fingers deep. It is important to fry at the correct temperature, which should be just before the oil reaches smoking point, 180°C/360°F. Add a drop of the batter and when it reaches the surface it is the moment to start adding the tortillitas.

Using a large spoon, add two or three tortillitas at the most in each batch as they should not touch. As the batter touches the oil, use the spoon to gently spread the batter to make each tortillita thinner and wider. When they take colour, turn once and cook until crisp and fluffy. Place the cooked tortillitas on kitchen paper to drain any excess oil, sprinkle with sea salt flakes then serve immediately while still piping hot.

Pimientos de Padrón
PADRÓN PEPPERS

These small, delicious green peppers are normally sweet but can also be surprisingly hot. They came to the Iberian Peninsula in the 16th century, all the way from Mexico. At first they were cultivated in Northern Galicia, probably by Franciscan monks, but in the last 30 years they have become very popular everywhere in Spain, including Andalucía. They can be deep fried or sautéed in olive oil, which is the way I love to prepare them. *(Pictured on page 32.)*

300 g/10½ oz. Pimientos de Padrón
  (Padrón peppers)
2–3 tablespoons Spanish extra virgin
  olive oil
sea salt flakes, to serve

SERVES 4

Using a colander wash the peppers under cold running water. Pat dry very well with kitchen paper and set aside.

Heat the oil in a frying pan/skillet and sauté the peppers for about 4–5 minutes or until they become very soft. Remove from the oil with a slotted spoon and place on kitchen pepper.

Serve piping hot sprinkled with sea salt flakes. Do not forget these as they make an enormous difference to the taste!

Aliñás
SUMMER POTATO SALAD

This is a truly refreshing summer salad and probably the most humble of all tapas but it is a recipe that calls for quality ingredients. In some local bars it is served for free on small white oval plates to accompany a drink. The secret resides not only in the combination of the ingredients (you should not use new or salad potatoes) but most importantly, when dressing the potatoes they should still be warm. At home we prepare this for lunch, adding a few pieces of canned albacore tuna fish in olive oil, which is very light in colour. It is perfect when served with egg mayonnaise, stuffed with the same tuna (see page 41) as well as other salads, such as a simple tomato salad dressed with good extra virgin olive oil and a sprinkle of oregano. *(Pictured on page 33)*

500 g/1 lb. 2 oz. potatoes, unpeeled
  (not new or salad potatoes)
1 small 185-g/6-oz. can albacore tuna,
  drained (optional)

FOR THE DRESSING
5 tablespoons Spanish extra virgin
  olive oil
3 tablespoons white wine vinegar
½ red onion or ½ large spring onion/
  scallion (*cebolleta*), chopped
a handful of fresh parsley, chopped
sea salt, to taste

SERVES 4

Boil the potatoes in their skins in a large pan of salted water. Meanwhile, prepare the dressing. Blend the oil with the vinegar, onions, parsley and salt in a small bowl. When the potatoes are tender, remove from the water, let them cool slightly, then peel off their skins. Chop the potatoes into irregular pieces and mix with the tuna (if using). Add more salt if needed, then pour over the dressing while the potatoes are warm.

Buñuelos de bacalao
SALT COD FRITTERS

Salt cod is as much a very popular ingredient in Andalucian cooking as it is in northern Spain. Some people desalt the fish at home but more and more it is bought in fishmongers and major retailers already 'desalinated' for the required recipe. Outside Spain it is easy to find in specialist Spanish and Portuguese shops.

1 kg/2¼ lb. potatoes, peeled
1 teaspoon unsalted butter
3 tablespoons whole/full-fat milk
2–3 tablespoons Spanish olive oil, plus extra for frying
½ white onion, chopped
2 garlic cloves, chopped
a handful of fresh parsley, chopped
250 g/9 oz. salt cod, desalinated (see page 82) and flaked
a pinch of sea salt, to taste
1 large/US extra-large egg, beaten
150 g/2 cups fine breadcrumbs, for coating

SERVES 6

Boil the potatoes in a large saucepan of water. When tender, remove from the water. Using a fork, mash the potatoes. Add the butter and milk and blend together. Reserve.

In a frying pan/skillet, heat the olive oil and sauté the onions and when they have taken some colour, add the garlic. Cook for 1 minute more at a moderate temperature. Reserve.

Add the parsley and the salt cod to the mashed potato and mix all together. Add the onion sofrito and blend well. Wet your hands with a little olive oil and roll small portions in your palms. Coat with beaten egg and then breadcrumbs. Fry in plenty of oil until golden in colour. Remove from the oil and pat dry with kitchen paper before serving while piping hot.

Gambas al ajillo
GARLIC PRAWNS

This is a classic tapas that is very popular in Andalucía. I am using what I consider to be the most traditional recipe, the one cooked without wine. I strongly recommend using fresh prawns/shrimp, but frozen ones, properly defrosted, can be a good alternative. Use medium or large prawns but never very small ones. In Aracena we have two excellent fishmongers who bring us amazing gambas daily from Huelva on the coast. It is great to serve them 'a la plancha' (from the grill) or in this case 'al ajillo' (with garlic). Serve this with the best artisan bread you can buy. Mopping the juices from the prawn and olive oil emulsion, the garlic and the chilli/chile make for an experience not to be missed! Any very dry white wine will be great here, but a *copita* or two of Manzanilla from Sanlúcar de Barrameda will bring a true taste of Andalucía to any moment of the day.

Spanish extra virgin olive oil, for frying
1 fresh or dried red chilli/chile pepper
   (medium heat), sliced
5 garlic cloves, sliced
500 g/1 lb. 2 oz. medium to large raw
   prawns/shrimp, peeled
sea salt and freshly ground black pepper,
   to season
good artisan bread, to serve

SERVES 4

In a flameproof dish or frying pan/skillet, heat about 2 fingers of olive oil over a medium heat. Add the chilli/chile pepper, followed by the garlic. Stir until the garlic takes a little colour. Increase the heat rapidly and add the prawns/shrimp. You may think there is too much olive oil but within a minute the prawns will release their juices and these will emulsify with it to make an opaque, light-coloured and aromatic liquor. Do not overcook. Serve hot accompanied by bread.

Queso con salsa de pimiento rojo, tomate y guindilla
FRESH CHEESE WITH SWEET PEPPER, TOMATO & CHILLI SAUCE

In Andalucía I made this recipe using a fresh goat cheese with a texture similar to halloumi, but it is less salty and slightly softer. The idea for the sauce came from my dear friend Carolina Muir, a talented cook who I first met years ago when teaching at a cookery school in Gaucín, not far from Ronda.

This is a fresh sauce, with a thin texture that should have a well-balanced taste between the heat of the fresh chilli/chile and the sugar. As it won't keep, prepare the sauce just for the recipe.

250 g/9 oz. *queso fresco*
   (or any fresh crumbly cheese), sliced
white maize flour, for dusting
Spanish olive oil, for frying

FOR THE SAUCE
1 red (bell) pepper, deseeded and
   chopped
1 fresh red chilli/chile (medium heat),
   deseeded and chopped
4 small ripe tomatoes, peeled
1 garlic clove, peeled
a little fresh ginger, peeled and grated
a small splash of red wine vinegar
caster/superfine sugar, to taste

SERVES 4

Place the red (bell) pepper, chilli/chile, tomatoes, garlic and ginger in an electric blender. Blend at a fast speed to a thin paste. Reduce the speed but while still running, add the vinegar and the sugar to taste. Set aside.

Coat the cheese slices with maize flour. Brush a small frying pan/skillet with olive oil and toast the cheese until it takes a light brownish colour. Serve hot with a little of the sauce drizzled over the top.

Mejillones gratinados rellenos de sofrito verduritas y salsa alioli

GRATINATED MUSSELS WITH SAUTÉED TOMATO, ONION & GREEN PEPPER STUFFING & ALIOLI SAUCE

Mussels stuffed with something delicious, topped with béchamel sauce, coated with breadcrumbs and fried (or cooked in the oven) are frequently offered in tapas bars. This recipe comes from a small bar in the city of Almería, in the province of the same name, rich in the production of vegetables as well as Mediterranean seafood. Here the chef had decided to do something different: to stuff mussels with a rich vegetable *sofrito* that pairs to perfection with an *alioli*.

For the purist, *alioli*, also known in Spanish as '*ajoaceite*' is made with garlic, olive oil and nothing else. This is a strong Mediterranean sauce, difficult to emulsify and maintain the emulsion intact. For these reasons, this recipe for stuffed mussels has been prepared with a simpler mayonnaise sauce with garlic. As we are using raw garlic cloves, I prefer to reduce their strength before they are added. One way to do this is to blanch the garlic in boiling water and the other is to microwave the garlic in their skins for just a few seconds.

1 kg/2¼ lb. fresh mussels, cleaned
a few handfuls of grated Manchego '*semicurado*' cheese (i.e. not too mature or strong), for topping

FOR THE SOFRITO
3 tablespoons Spanish olive oil
1 white onion, finely chopped
1 large green (bell) pepper, deseeded and finely chopped
500 g/1 lb. 2 oz. ripe tomatoes, peeled, deseeded and chopped
sea salt, to taste

FOR THE ALIOLI SAUCE
2 medium/US large egg yolks
2 garlic cloves
150 ml/⅔ cup sunflower oil
50 ml/3½ tablespoons Spanish olive oil
a pinch of sea salt
freshly squeezed lemon juice, to taste

SERVES 6

Steam the mussels in a large saucepan or stockpot. When open, remove from the pan and set aside to cool. When cool, keep each mussel sitting inside one half of the shell, discarding the other shell half. Place in one layer in an ovenproof dish.

To prepare the sofrito, heat the oil in a frying pan/skillet and sauté the onion until transparent. Add the peppers and sauté for a few minutes more before adding the tomatoes. Season with salt, then continue to cook, stirring frequently, until small oil bubbles appear on the surface.

To prepare the alioli sauce, place the egg yolks, a pinch of salt, the garlic and both oils in the tall container of a handheld blender. Insert the blender, and without moving from the bottom, start blending very fast until all the ingredients have emulsified almost completely. You can then move it up the container to emulsify any oil left at the top. Adjust the seasoning and add the lemon juice to taste. It will take about 30 seconds.

Preheat the oven to 180°C/160°C fan/350°F/Gas 4.

Place a teaspoon of sofrito on top of each mussel, carefully spoon the alioli on top and sprinkle some cheese over to finish. Cook in the preheated oven just for a few minutes until they take on some colour. Serve while hot.

Patatas arrugadas 'de Casa Juanito' con mojo picón

CASA JUANITO'S WRINKLY POTATOES WITH CANARIAN RED PEPPER SAUCE

This recipe originated in the Canary Islands where the Caribbean and South American influence is easy to find. I have enjoyed '*arrugadas*' on the islands of Tenerife and Gran Canaria and yet the best version of this dish I have had was the main attraction of Casa Juanito, a restaurant in Isla Cristina in the province of Huelva. Here the connection with the Americas is also strong. The dish is always served accompanied with a number of sauces they call '*mojos*', including the spicy *mojo picón*. The potato inside of the skin interestingly does not become salty. This is a perfect party dish and excellent '*tapa*' or '*ración*'. It is always good and always very popular.

1 kg/2¼ lb. small salad potatoes, unpeeled
100 g/½ cup coarse sea salt

FOR THE MOJO PICÓN
2 garlic cloves, sliced
1 teaspoon cumin seeds
½ fresh red chilli/chile pepper (medium heat), deseeded and chopped
½ sweet red (bell) pepper
½ teaspoon *pimentón picante* (Spanish hot paprika)
120 ml/½ cup sunflower oil
20 ml/4 teaspoons white wine vinegar
sea salt, to taste

SERVES 4–6

Make the Mojo Picón first. Place the garlic and a pinch of salt in a mortar and use the pestle to pound to a paste. Add the cumin seeds and pound again. Add the chilli/chile pepper, followed by the sweet (bell) pepper and pound. Add the pimentón and blend with the rest of the ingredients before starting to pour the oil in, adding it drop by drop. Work with the pestle. The sauce will start to emulsify. Flavour the sauce with the vinegar and adjust the salt if necessary.

To prepare the potatoes use a large saucepan with a heavy lid and place the potatoes in one layer if possible. Add the salt and just cover with cold water. As the potatoes should cook with steam, cover the saucepan first with a clean heavy kitchen cloth, then with the lid and with another cloth on top. They should be ready within 30 minutes. By then the water will have evaporated, leaving the salt attached to the skin of the potatoes. If any liquid remains cover the saucepan with the lid, place it on the heat again and shake the pan several times.

Serve the Mojo Picón on the side and dip each hot salty potato into the sauce as you eat.

Huevos con salsa mahonesa y bonito
EGGS STUFFED WITH TUNA MAYONNAISE

These can be a very average or a lovely summer dish, but to be a great dish it requires time in the kitchen. The secret rests with the quality of all the ingredients used. I recommend making a handmade Salsa Mahonesa and to use a good quality light tuna (*albacore*) or a *bonito en escabeche* (see page 110), which is sold in cans preserved in vegetable oil or, even better, Spanish extra virgin olive oil.

9 medium/US large eggs
2–3 x 113-g/4-oz. cans white tuna fish
    in olive oil, drained and flaked
30 g/1 cup fresh parsley, very finely
    chopped
1 recipe Salsa Mahonesa
    (see recipe right)
sea salt and freshly ground black pepper

SERVES 6

Boil the eggs in a saucepan of water for 10 minutes, then refresh under cold running water. Remove the shells and cut in half. Scoop out the yolks and place them in a mixing bowl. Season with salt and pepper, add the tuna and some of the parsley and mix together. Add some Salsa Mahonesa to the blend and mix through – don't take too much, as you need the rest it later.

Use a spoon to stuff the egg whites with small portions of the egg yolk mixture and place them in a flat serving dish. Cover with the rest of the Salsa Mahonesa and sprinkle with the remaining parsley just before serving.

NOTE *I normally serve these accompanied with the Warm Spicy Carrot Salad with Mint on page 87.*

Salsa mahonesa
MAYONNAISE

This *Salsa Mahonesa* is an important addition to some dishes which have been included in this book, such as the *Gazpachuelo Malagueño* (see page 98) and the *Huevos con Salsa Mahonesa y Bonito* (see recipe left). Although it is easy to make this sauce using a stick electric blender, I often prepare my *Salsa Mahonesa* by hand, I find that the texture and flavour are superior. While I prefer to use sunflower oil I recommend using a small amount of Spanish olive oil as well, although it should not be strong in flavour, as olive oil imparts something special to the sauce.

Make certain that all the ingredients are at the same temperature before you begin preparation and that the eggs you are using are very fresh.

2 large/US extra-large egg yolks
freshly squeezed juice of ½ a lemon
150 ml/scant ⅔ cup sunflower oil
20 ml/4 teaspoons Spanish olive oil
white wine vinegar, to taste (optional)
1 tablespoon warm water
sea salt and ground white pepper

MAKES 200 G/1 CUP

In a large deep bowl, whisk the egg yolks together with a pinch of salt and a few drops of lemon juice. Work fast until well blended. Add a pinch of white pepper. Using a jug/pitcher, and without stopping, start adding the oil, little by little – first the sunflower oil, followed by the olive oil. As it takes quite some time and the hand and arm get tired, whisk in both directions and change hands when required. Adjust the seasoning if needed, adding a few drops of warm water and a few more of lemon juice (or white wine vinegar) to taste. The emulsion will become slightly lighter and whiter. Cover and chill until needed.

BREADS

Bread & Rice

Amongst 'all things food', it is fair to say that all Spaniards share a love of both bread and rice.

When talking about Spanish rice, we tend to think only of Paella and the rice dishes associated with the east coast of Spain (Valencia, Alicante and Murcia), often referred to as the Spanish Levante. In this area, rice is almost a way of living and yet we have to remember that Andalucía is infact Spain's main producer of rice and that rice dishes are very popular here too. As a lover of rice, who could eat rice every single day of the year, I am always on the hunt for great rice dishes and in Andalucía I have found and enjoyed many diverse recipes. This book includes a number of those that I have encountered over the years spent exploring southern Spain.

Some are cooked in a paella pan, although they are not the classic and authentic *Paella Valenciana*. In Andalucía, dogma and rice don't go together, it is simply left to the cook, even if, as in Valencia, the

rice dishes can be cooked *seco* (dry), *meloso* (the consistency of an Italian risotto) or *caldoso* (soupy).

The late José Antonio Valdespino, owner of the legendary restaurant *La Mesa Redonda en Jerez*, spoke vehemently about the amazing rice dishes cooked in western Andalucía with duck and vegetables produced in the dunes area of Cádiz known as *Los Navazos* where fabulous vegetables are grown in the sand. *Arroz con Pollo* (Rice with Chicken) is very popular everywhere (see page 134 for *Paula's Arroz con Pollo*), while the *Arroz con Marisco* cooked by Fernando Bigote in Sanlúcar de Barrameda is one of the most tasty *arroces caldosos* to be found in the Costas. Traditionally the *caldosos* are cooked in *cazuelas* (earthenware pots). There are two more

dishes I would like to add to this list, the *Arroz a la Sevillana en Paella* (see page 114) which contains chorizo, jamón, monkfish and squid, among other ingredients, and the *Arroz de Rabo de Toro y Boletus* (Rice with Oxtail and Boletus) which I prepare in early Spring in El Zauzal following the traditional recipe from Córdoba. At that time of the year boletus and other wild mushrooms are found all over the Sierras.

Moving onto bread, it would be difficult to find a Spaniard who does not like good bread or to understand 'the Spanish table' without it. It is in Galicia, but especially in Andalucía, where I have consistently found some of the most tasty and varied breads in the whole of the country. Having lived mostly in Madrid for the first part of my life, I grew up eating, as all *madrileños* did, a kind of boring white bread known as a *pistola* (pistol), the name given to a sort of baguette of little distinction baked 'to kill hunger' during the Franco era. It was during the summers,

while enjoying our holidays in other parts of the country, where we could enjoy the kind of good bread I can now buy everywhere in Andalucía. What I love most is that bread is getting better all the time. Bakers are responding to the appreciation of both their new and existing customers, all of whom are prepared to pay a premium for better quality bread.

One thing we all appreciated when we first spent time in our house in Aracena, was the quality of the bread there, but it was almost just one type of white bread made into different shapes. It was good bread but nothing particularly exciting, though it pleased the majority of the population. Then, a couple of years ago something miraculous happened. A bakery and excellent supplier of pulses/legumes, wines and olive oil, *El Molinillo* opened its doors in the centre of Aracena, selling excellent *barras de pan* in the shape of the much-maligned *pistola*, as well as especially good-looking and irresistible *Hogaza* (see page 46) made with a selection of grains that had become difficult to find locally. Since then the queues outside of the shop speak loudly about the success of the 'best bakery in town'. As well as the hogaza, when I am in the shop, I buy *Molletes Andaluces* (see page 49) as a treat for the next morning's breakfast.

Hogaza 'de Siempre'
HOGAZA, AN ANDALUCIAN LOAF

I use a baking stone to bake this crisp, crusted and spongy textured bread that is popular in Andalucía and many other parts of Spain.
Begin by preparing the starter dough the night before you wish to bake the loaf.

FOR THE STARTER
7 g/¼ oz. dried yeast
85 ml/⅓ cup tepid water and probably a little more
170 g/1¼ cups plain/all-purpose flour
Spanish olive oil, for greasing

FOR THE DOUGH
10 g/⅓ oz. dried yeast
250 ml/1 cup tepid water
250 g/1¾ cups strong flour, plus extra for dusting
150 g/1 generous cup stoneground wholemeal/whole-wheat flour
8 g/1½ teaspoons salt
Spanish olive oil, for greasing

MAKES 1 LOAF TO SHARE

To make the starter dough, dissolve the yeast in 2–3 tablespoons of the tepid water. Place the flour in a bowl with the yeast and add the remaining water a little at the time, mixing it in very lightly with your hands. You may need a little more water to handle the dough more easily. Transfer the dough to your working surface and brush with some olive oil. Knead for about 10 minutes or until smooth and elastic. Grease a bowl with a little olive oil, place the dough in the bowl and cover with a damp dish towel. Set aside in a cool place or the fridge to rise overnight.

For the second dough, place the yeast in a large mixing bowl with a couple of tablespoons of the tepid water. Stir to dissolve, then leave it to rest for about 5 minutes. Add the starter dough and mix well until blended. Add the flours and salt in several batches, incorporating each addition well before adding the next. Once evenly mixed, tip the dough on to a floured work surface and knead for 10–15 minutes or until smooth and elastic.

Place the dough in an oiled bowl, oiling the surface of the dough to prevent a skin forming. Cover and leave to rise at room temperature, or slightly cooler, for 3 hours or until it has doubled in bulk.

Punch the dough to knock out any air and turn to a lightly floured surface. Knead briefly, and form into a round loaf. Slash the top in a cross at the top with a very sharp knife. Place on a floured baking sheet, cover with a clean kitchen towel and leave it to rise at room temperature for about 1 hour, or until doubled in size.

About 30 minutes before you are ready to bake, preheat the oven to the highest temperature with a baking stone inside if you have one, or a baking sheet if you don't.

When the bread has risen, slide it onto the hot stone or baking sheet. Reduce the oven temperature to 220°C/200°C fan/425°F/Gas 7 and bake for 40–50 minutes or until light golden and well risen. The bread should sound hollow when tapped on the base. Leave to cool on a wire rack before slicing to serve.

Molletes Andaluces

ANDALUCIAN BREAD ROLLS WITH TOMATOES, OLIVE OIL & IBÉRICO HAM

The word '*mollete*' is a generic name given to different breads in the whole of Spain and in South America. In Andalucía they are eaten for breakfast at home every day or in restaurants and bars and always toasted. Andalucians love these simply sprinkled with extra virgin olive oil and sea salt or even better, with a sauce of fresh tomatoes with or without Ibérico ham on top. The most renowned ones come from the town of Antequera in the Málaga region.

2–3 large tomatoes
Spanish extra virgin olive oil,
    for drizzling
sea salt, to taste
Ibérico ham, to serve (optional)

FOR THE STARTER
3 g/½ teaspoon fresh yeast
75 ml/scant ⅓ cup tepid water
75 g/½ cup plain/all-purpose flour,
    plus extra for dusting

FOR THE DOUGH
475 g/3½ cups medium strong
    flour, sifted
7 g/¼ oz. fine sea salt
25 g/¾ oz. pork lard, broken into
    small pieces, at room temperature
2 g/½ teaspoon fresh yeast

*a baking dish lined with baking
    paper*

MAKES 10

To prepare the sourdough starter, dissolve the fresh yeast in tepid water. Place the flour in a mixing bowl and add the dissolved yeast. Using your fingers, work it together for a few minutes, then shape into a ball. Cover with a clean cloth and leave it to rise for 10–12 hours in a warm place.

To make the dough, in a large bowl, mix 270 ml/1 cup plus 2 tablespoons water with the flour, little by little. Working with your fingers or using two spatulas, knead to obtain a homogeneous elastic dough that is difficult to handle. Add the ball of starter dough and the salt. Still in the bowl, carry on kneading until it is possible to form a larger ball. Helped by the spatulas, place the dough on a surface sprinkled with flour. Knead for another 10 minutes to a more consistent dough, while incorporating the lard. Reserve the dough in another large bowl that has been lightly coated with oil. Cover with a clean cloth and leave it to rise in a warm place for another hour.

Preheat the oven to 240°C/220°C fan/450°F/Gas 8. Place the dough on the floured surface again, and patting lightly with your knuckles, remove some of the air. Knead again into a ball. Divide the dough into 10 equal portions and with the tips of your fingers, shape each one into flat round shapes before placing in the prepared baking dish. Bake in the preheated oven for 10–12 minutes until they are light in colour.

Grate the tomatoes to a pulp over a bowl. Pour in the olive oil and season to taste with salt.

Once the molletes have baked and cooled, split each one open, spread with the tomato sauce, drizzle with olive oil and serve with Ibérico ham, if liked.

Empanadillas de atún con pimientos rojos y cebolla asados

ROAST PEPPER, ONION & TUNA EMPANADILLAS

My mother often made us *empanadillas*. She served them hot, to eat for lunch or dinner with a salad and *patatas fritas* (chips/fries), piping hot from the pan. We all adored these tantalizing small pies and they have remained an unforgettable food memory from my childhood, especially as part of mother's picnic basket: potato *tortilla*, roasted chicken legs, her special potato salad we called *ensaladilla de mama*, a good plate of Serrano ham and, of course, her delicious *Empanadillas de Atún*, which are equally good when cold. Sometimes she would fry them and at other times she would bake them in the oven, I do the same. The dough is easy to make but you can buy it in shops already prepared under the brand *La Molinera*.

2 large red (bell) peppers, left whole
2 large white onions, halved
2 x 115-g/4-oz. cans tuna fish fillets in extra virgin olive oil (ventresca if available), flaked
Spanish olive oil, for coating and frying
sea salt

FOR THE DOUGH
300 g/2¼ cups plain/all-purpose flour, plus extra for dusting
1 teaspoon salt
30 ml/2 tablespoons sunflower oil
150 ml/⅔ cup hot water
beaten egg, if needed

a rolling pin
a round 10-cm/4-inch pastry cutter

MAKES 8–10

Preheat the oven to 180°C/160°C fan/350°F/Gas 4.

Coat the vegetables with olive oil using your hands. Place the whole peppers and the halved onions in a roasting pan. Sprinkle with salt and roast for 30–40 minutes, turning several times, until tender. When cool, remove the skins from the peppers and onions and chop the flesh together. Transfer to a bowl and mix coarsely with the tuna. Taste and adjust the seasoning with more salt if needed.

Meanwhile, in a bowl, mix the flour, salt and oil and add the hot water. Work first with a spatula and then with your hands to make a ball. Add a little more water if needed. Cover the bowl with cling film/plastic wrap and place in the fridge for about 30–40 minutes. Sprinkle the work surface with flour, roll the dough out with the rolling pin until very thin. Using the pastry cutter, cut out 8–10 discs, rerolling the trimmings as necessary.

Before filling the empanadillas, moisten the outside of the pastry discs with a little water using your finger. Fill one half the pastry base with some of the vegetable and tuna mixture, making certain there is space to fold over the pastry top. Press down the edges with the tines of a fork to seal and contain the filling.

Increase the oven temperature to 200°C/180°C fan/400°F/Gas 6.

Brush the empanadillas with beaten egg if liked, and bake in the preheated oven for about 12 minutes, turning several times, until golden and crisp.

NOTE *You can also deep fry these empanadillas in plenty of oil heated to around 170°C/338°F, turning frequently until golden all over.*

Saladillas típicas de Granada
CELEBRATION BREADS FROM GRANADA

On 3rd May every year, the city of Granada celebrates *El Día de la Cruz* (The Day of the Cross). This ancient festival is a fusion of religious beliefs in Spain and South America. In Granada it has become a very colourful day with broad/ fava beans and salted cod *saladillas* offered in restaurants and bars, with music and dancing in the streets. The rising of the dough for these takes the time it takes, but the kneading can be made faster using a food processor fitted with a dough hook.

500 g/3½–3⅔ cups strong flour, sifted, plus extra for dusting
3 g/½ teaspoon of dried yeast, for breadmaking
300 ml/1¼ cups warm water
2 tablespoons Spanish olive oil, plus extra for drizzling
½ teaspoon sea salt flakes

MAKES 2 BREADS TO SHARE

Place the flour and yeast in a bowl, blend and add the warm water. Mix together. Still in the bowl, and using one hand, start kneading until the dough becomes very elastic and continue for 4 minutes. Cover with a clean kitchen cloth and leave to rest for 30 minutes.

Knead it a little more to remove the air. Then add the olive oil. Knead again until all the olive oil has been completely absorbed. Leave it to rest for another 30 minutes.

Remove the air once more. Cover again and let it rest for another 30 minutes.

Sprinkle flour over the work surface, place the dough on top and start kneading properly with both hands. Leave it to rest for another 30 minutes.

Preheat the oven to 220°C/200°C fan/425°F/Gas 7.

Kneading it again, take out the air for the last time. Cut the dough in half. Place a piece of baking paper on the work surface and flatten the dough with the fingers of both hands, extending the dough into a circle. Cover and let it rest for a little longer. With your index fingers punch small indentations all over the surface. Sprinkle sea salt flakes all over and pour drops of olive oil into each dent. Bake in the preheated oven for 15 minutes, until pale golden.

Picos Sevillanos
LITTLE CRUNCHY BREADS FOR TAPAS

In Andalucía, many tapas plates come accompanied by little pieces of crunchy dried breads that can be made at home or bought in food shops. Never larger than a small finger, and of similar shape, they are very versatile, easy to make and can be kept for several weeks.

The origin of these breads goes back to the 15th and 16th centuries in Spain. Picos are associated with the food eaten by sailors during the neverending voyages across the Atlantic Ocean.

FOR THE STARTER
3 g/½ teaspoon dried yeast
warm water
75 g/½ cup plain/all-purpose flour
30 g/3½ tablespoons bread flour

FOR THE DOUGH
2 g/a pinch of dried yeast
400 g/3 cups plain/all-purpose flour
100 g/¾ cup bread flour
200 ml/scant 1 cup warm water
50 ml/scant ¼ cup Spanish olive oil, plus extra for brushing
6 g/1 teaspoon fine sea salt

MAKES ABOUT 100

To prepare the starter, dissolve the yeast in a cup with a little warm water. When frothing add to the flours in a bowl along with 50 ml/scant ¼ cup water. Work first with a small spatula and then with your fingers, kneading gently to a fairly elastic dough. Knead the dough into a ball. Cover the bowl with clingfilm/plastic wrap and chill overnight in the fridge.

For the dough, dissolve the dried yeast in a cup with a little warm water. Then in a large bowl blend in this dissolved dried yeast with the flours, warm water, oil, salt and the starter. As with making the starter, work first with a spatula and then with your fingers until all the ingredients are almost integrated. On your work surface, start kneading until the dough becomes elastic. Knead this into a ball and place back in the bowl and brush with olive oil. Cover this bowl with clingfilm/plastic wrap. Let the dough ferment for a couple or hours. Place it back on the work surface and knead to remove the air. Form again into a ball.

Cut the ball into quarters and roll into thick sticks. Start cutting small pieces of equal size (about 5–6 g/¼ oz. each) from the sticks. Shape into little balls with your hands and then roll each ball into a small finger shape. Let them rest for 1 hour. Spread the picos out in a single layer on a baking sheet (you will need to bake in two batches).

Preheat the oven to 180°C/160°C fan/350°F/Gas 4.

For the perfect picos, I recommend you put a deep dish of hot water in the oven on the bottom shelf. Bake the picos for about 8 minutes. Remove the bowl of water and bake for another 15 minutes. Switch off the oven, open the door and leave the picos in the oven to get crunchy for another 10 minutes. Serve once cooled. These will store in an airtight container for up to 2–3 weeks.

NOTE *As this dough makes quite a large portion, I often divide it in half and freeze, so that I can make a second batch of picos another time.*

Tortas de aceite y anís
SWEET OLIVE OIL & ANISEED 'TORTAS'

Whether you make these crisp tortas at home (they are very easy to make) or you buy them in a shop (Ines Rosales is an excellent brand), they can be eaten at any time. Crisp, imbued with just the right amount of sweetness and a hint of aniseed, they are truly moreish!

100 ml/⅓ cup Spanish extra virgin olive oil
1 tablespoon aniseeds
1 tablespoon sesame seeds
500 g/3½–3⅔ cups strong flour, sifted
75 g/⅓ cup white sugar, plus extra for sprinkling
25 g/1½ tablespoons brown sugar
1 teaspoon ground cinnamon
10 g/2 teaspoons baking powder
1 tablespoon *Anís del Mono Dulce* (Spanish sweet aniseed liqueur) or a sweet dessert wine
½ teaspoon sea salt
1 egg white, beaten

a large baking sheet, lined with baking paper

MAKES ABOUT 15

Preheat the oven to 180°C/160°C fan/350°F/Gas 4.

Heat the olive oil in a small saucepan. When hot but not smoky, add the aniseed and sesame seeds, stir and leave them to infuse the oil. Set aside.

Place the flour in a large mixing bowl. Make a space in the centre and start adding the white and brown sugars, cinnamon, baking powder and the anis liqueur or wine. Blend everything together well with a wooden spoon. Add the infused olive oil, by then it should be cold, followed by 150 ml/⅔ cup water. Stir again to fully integrate.

Once the dough starts taking consistency, transfer to the work surface. Start kneading for several minutes to make a ball. Take portions of about 40 g/1½ oz. each and use your hands to shape into small balls. Next using first your hand and then a small rolling pin, shape into thin circles.

Place the tortas on the prepared baking sheet. Brush with the egg white and sprinkle with a little sugar. Bake for about 10 minutes or until they start taking colour. Remove from the oven and let cool – they will become quite crisp and very delicious. These will store in an airtight container for 1-2 weeks.

VEGETABLES
ALL YEAR
AROUND

Vegetables & More

I am not quite sure when I first started travelling in Andalucía but it must be certainly more that 30 years ago. What I do remember is that it was winter and I was taking a group of British journalists to visit an olive oil *almazara* (mill) in the province of Córdoba, in Baena. It was raining and it was cold. Within minutes of entering the main building, in true Andalucian style we found ourselves in a large traditional room with a welcoming fire and a cup of warming chicken and vegetable broth in our hands. It had been made by the mother of our host who was already in the kitchen preparing lunch. Having had a tour of the extensive olive grove and a tasting of olive oil from the new crop, we sat inside another large building full of old *tinajas* (earthenware amphorae), all painted in white and green, not in use but decorative and evocative. Here, our lunch was laid out ready to be served. On the table were marinated olives, home-baked *Hogaza* (see page 46) and a bottle of a very distinctive olive oil. What followed was a food

journey to remember. We started lunch with a plate of the sweetest oranges picked from the garden, drizzled with amazing olive oil and local honey. As a first course we had a bowl of chickpeas with spinach, followed by a tasty chicken cooked with sun-dried red (bell) peppers, tomatoes and herbs. The dessert proved to be something entirely new, an unusual ice cream made with the lightest and sweetest olive oil that surprisingly worked extremely well!

Andalucía has been a great producer of fresh vegetables and fruits, as well as grains, since early history. The Romans selected old Hispania to supply their legions with grain to make bread and olive oil to fry fish as well as to beautify themselves. Equally important were grapes for making wine which was shipped in large quantities to Italy. It was plentiful and cheaper. Much later by the 10th century the 'Moors,' the generic name given to the Islamic warriors, traders and superb agriculturists (both Arab and Berber), had already done a serious rescue job in Andalucía and

in the rest of Al-Andalus, the name they gave to the Iberian Peninsula. They improved irrigation systems originally installed by the Romans centuries before. They brought with them a range of new crops and products to enrich the land and the *cocina* (cuisine). They planted rice by the Guadalquivir river, bitter oranges to decorate and perfume the streets in cities and towns, they also brought grapefruit, spinach and cardoons, melons and watermelons among many others. With a very sweet tooth they made certain that sugar cane planted in the cities of Málaga, Granada and Sevilla would become both an economic and a culinary success. It is true to say that Moorish culinary traditions and agricultural knowledge did not reach and influence everywhere in the Iberian peninsula to quite the same extent, however it is also true that in the 'Cocina Andaluza' whether modern or traditional, Moorish heritage is very much alive. Look how often spices from the Orient introduced by the Moors are included in many recipes cooked today.

Fresh and dried herbs are also an important ingredient in the *Cocina Andaluza*. Rosemary is added to small game dishes as well as lamb and pork; thyme for stews of meat and fish and with summer vegetables. Andalucians love fresh fennel in meat and vegetable stews and with fish – fennel seeds are also very popular in marinades. Parsley is used for almost everything; marjoram is favoured with game, lamb dishes and stuffing; oregano (my favourite herb) accentuates the unique taste of tomato salads and dishes cooked with pork. Basil, which is known as names, *albahaca*, is also excellent in tomato salads. Bay leaf which, in my opinion should be used in moderation, adds something special to vegetable stews, to chicken and to marinades. Finally, mint, which is rarely used in the rest of Spain, is just wonderful with cold and hot soups and with fruit and other desserts as well as in many other local specialities.

Gazpacho Andaluz
ANDALUCIAN GAZPACHO

Gazpacho in Andalucía began centuries ago as a light soup made with stale bread softened with water and flavoured with oil, garlic and vinegar. Later, more sophisticated gazpachos made with almonds became popular in Málaga and Córdoba. With the arrival of the tomato, green (bell) pepper and cucumber from the Americas, a more colourful and fresher version became a staple of the Andalucian kitchen, especially in summer.

When flavoursome tomatoes are not available you can greatly enhance the flavour of the gazpacho by macerating the vegetables already chopped and all the rest of the ingredients for at least 2–3 hours, or better overnight, before blending. To obtain the texture Andalucians consider the best, which is slightly grainy, gazpachos used to be prepared using a pestle and mortar but today the electric blender does a good job.

50 g/1¾ oz. stale bread, crusts removed and crumbled
1 kg/2¼ lb. ripe, tasty tomatoes, chopped
1 green (bell) pepper, deseeded and chopped
1–2 garlic cloves, peeled
1 cucumber, peeled and sliced, plus a little extra, diced, to serve
100 ml/scant ½ cup Spanish extra virgin olive oil
2–3 tablespoons sherry vinegar
sea salt
very cold water, for topping up

SERVES 6

NOTE *Gazpacho should be served very cold however to my taste it does not need ice before serving. As it melts, ice dilutes the concentration of the vegetables and therefore flavour.*

Soak the bread in some water and when well-soaked, squeeze the water out.

Place the tomatoes, green (bell) pepper, garlic, cucumber and bread in a food processor or blender. Start blending to a creamy consistency, adding the olive oil, little by little. Season and add vinegar to taste. Add cold water until the desired consistency is reached and blend again. Place in the fridge until ready to serve, garnished with diced cucumber.

Pipirrana de Jaén
SUMMER SALAD FROM JAÉN

This is a recipe to prepare when tomatoes are in season, as the tasty juices of ripe tomatoes will make a great difference to the taste of the dish. This is a traditional salad from Jaén but it is also prepared in Córdoba and Granada. It is a salad that would never be served without good bread, which is needed to mop up all the lovely juices.

1 garlic clove, chopped
1 egg, hard-boiled/cooked,
   then separated
1 green (bell) pepper, deseeded
   and chopped
Spanish extra virgin olive oil, to taste
2 large ripe tomatoes, peeled and
   chopped (juices reserved)
½ large spring onion/scallion
   (cebolleta), chopped
sea salt

SERVES 4

Place the garlic in a mortar with a little salt and using a pestle pound to a paste. Add the hard-boiled/cooked egg yolk and carry on pounding before adding half the green (bell) pepper. Pound again and start to add the oil to taste (starting with a couple of tablespoons) and a little water to loosen. Reserve.

Chop the egg white and set aside.

Place the tomatoes in a bowl with all the juices, the rest of the green pepper, the spring onion/scallion and the hard-boiled egg white. Mix well before adding the dressing. Season with salt.

Cover with clingfilm/plastic wrap and place in the fridge at least for 3–4 hours for the vegetables to release more juices, which will make this simple dish into something very refreshing and easy to prepare.

Ensalada de naranja, miel y aceite de oliva
ORANGE, HONEY & OLIVE OIL SALAD

Often you will see toasted bread with fresh tomatoes, sprinkled with olive oil and a little sea salt, served for breakfast in bars and hotels in Andalucía. At home in Aracena, it is always on our breakfast table for those who like something a little different. However, in winter I love to serve a plate with fresh oranges picked from the garden, drizzled with olive oil from a local mill, as well as honey from the bee hives of our local producer **María José Moreno.** *(Pictured on page 1.)*

4 medium oranges
3 teaspoons runny honey
freshly squeezed juice of ½ an orange
3 tablespoons Spanish extra virgin
   olive oil
a few fresh mint leaves, to garnish

SERVES 4

Cut away all the skin and pith from the oranges and using a serrated knife, cut each orange into 5–6 thin slices. Arrange the fruit on a large serving plate.

Blend the honey with the orange juice in a small bowl, then drizzle over the fruit, followed by the olive oil. Garnish with a few mint leaves to add extra flavour and freshness and serve.

Bastoncitos de berenjena con salmorejo

AUBERGINE BATONS COATED IN MAIZE FLOUR, SERVED WITH SALMOREJO SAUCE

Cádiz is a truly ancient city to admire particularly when crossing the old part to reach the historical sea walls facing the Atlantic Ocean and the romantic *Barrio de la Viña*, where a number of bars and restaurants serve this dish. Salmorejo is a thick flavoursome gazpacho from Córdoba that is used as a sauce in this recipe.

2 medium aubergines/eggplants
maize flour, for coating
Spanish olive oil, for frying
sea salt

FOR THE SALMOREJO SAUCE
1 kg/2¼ lb. very ripe tomatoes,
  just out of the fridge, peeled
  and chopped
1–2 garlic cloves, chopped
200 g/7 oz. white bread, at least
  a day old, soaked in water,
  then drained
150 ml/⅔ cup Spanish olive oil
a drizzle of sherry vinegar
sea salt and freshly ground black
  pepper, to season

SERVES 4

Fresh aubergines/eggplants are slightly bitter. To remove their bitterness cut each one into 4 lengthways, sprinkle with salt and leave them to rest for about 30 minutes.

Meanwhile, prepare the Salmorejo Sauce. Place the tomatoes, garlic, bread and a little cold water in a food processor or blender. Blend, then start adding the olive oil, very slowly, until it becomes emulsified. Add the vinegar, season with salt and pepper and add 2–3 tablespoons warm water if needed to achieve the desired consistency. Pour the sauce into 4 small individual serving dishes and set aside at room temperature.

Wash the aubergines gently in running water to remove excess salt. Pat dry with kitchen paper and cut into long, thick batons (*bastoncitos*) as equal in size as possible.

Heat plenty of olive oil in a large frying pan/skillet, coat the bastoncitos with the maize flour. Fry in batches for a few minutes each time, until golden in colour. Pat dry again on kitchen paper and serve piping hot with the Salmorejo Sauce on the side for dipping.

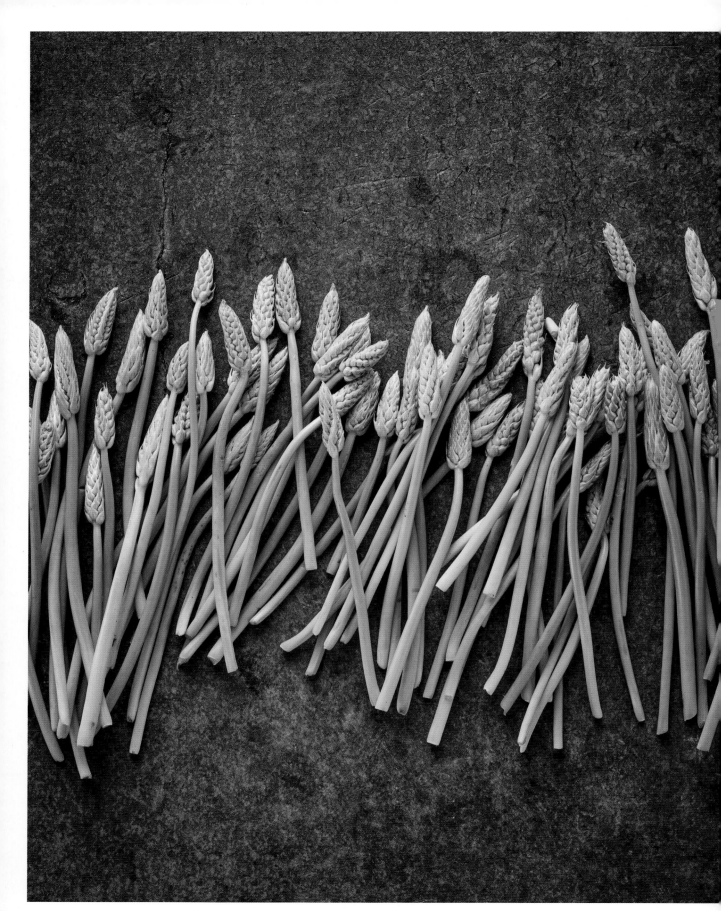

Láminas de alcachofas y espárragos trigueros con salsa 'al ajo verde'

ARTICHOKE & WILD ASPARAGUS WITH GREEN GARLIC SAUCE

Springtime is a good time of the year to prepare any recipes with artichokes and wild or cultivated green asparagus. Here I have chosen to share a special sauce, *Ajo Verde*, that brings an extra dimension to vegetables, grilled meat or fish dishes.
(Pictured on page 71.)

1 lemon, for squeezing
8 medium artichokes
20 thin green asparagus spears

FOR THE AJO VERDE SAUCE
1 egg white
2 garlic cloves, sliced
20 g/1 cup finely snipped chives
30 g/¼ cup pistachio kernels
freshly squeezed juice of 1 lemon
50 g/1 cup fresh breadcrumbs
10 g/½ cup freshly chopped parsley
    leaves
200 ml/generous ¾ cup Spanish
    extra virgin olive oil
fine sea salt and ground white
    pepper, to season

SERVES 4

Fill a medium bowl with plenty of fresh water and add a few squeezes of lemon juice.

Remove the stalks and outer leaves from the artichokes. Use a spoon to remove the fibrous centre of the artichokes to avoid darkening and place them in the lemon water. Set aside.

In a large saucepan, bring plenty of water to the boil, add a little lemon juice and salt. To maintain the temperature of the water, add the artichokes one by one. Cook them all together until tender. Remove from the heat and let them cool down in the liquid.

Cook the asparagus in a saucepan of salted boiling water. Do not overcook as it should retain a little bite. Set aside and leave to cool.

Prepare the Ajo Verde in an electric blender (I use a Thermomix). Add the egg white, then the garlic, chives, pistachio kernels, lemon juice, breadcrumbs, parsley, 120 ml/½ cup water and some salt and white pepper. With the machine running, start adding the olive oil, little by little, until the sauce becomes very glossy and is neither too thin nor too thick.

Before serving, gently pat the artichokes and the asparagus dry and carefully slice the artichokes, not too thin. Serve in a flat dish with the Ajo Verde sauce spooned over the top.

Olla gitana
GYPSY'S HOT POT

From time to time I have to defend Spanish vegetarian food. Many people believe it does not exist; too much chorizo, too much ham they say. This 'olla', one of the names given in Andalucía to numerous vegetarian and non-vegetarian stews, is one of my favourite meat-free recipes.

The recipe can be prepared with dried or already pre-soaked chickpeas/garbanzo beans which are sold in glass jars. There are a number of good Spanish brands on the market. (*Pictured on page 75.*)

250 g/1½ cups dried or pre-soaked chickpeas/garbanzo beans
1 teaspoon bicarbonate of soda/baking soda
250 g/9 oz. green beans, cut into 3-cm/1¼-in. pieces
150 g/5½ oz. pumpkin, peeled and cut into cubes
3 pears, peeled, cored and quartered
1 white onion, chopped
100 ml/scant ½ cup Spanish olive oil
1 teaspoon *pimentón dulce* (Spanish sweet paprika)
2 ripe large tomatoes, peeled and chopped
1 small slice of bread
1 garlic clove
10 raw almonds, toasted and peeled
6–7 saffron filaments, dissolved in a little hot water
1 tablespoon red wine vinegar
sea salt and freshly ground black pepper, to season

SERVES 6–8

To prepare this recipe in the traditional way with dried chickpeas/garbanzo beans, soak them overnight in plenty of water with the bicarbonate of soda/baking soda to tenderize. In the morning, rinse in a colander under cold running water.

In a large saucepan, bring plenty of water to the boil and add the soaked chickpeas/garbanzo beans. Cover and simmer gently for about 1 hour or until tender.

Add the green beans, pumpkin and pears and continue to simmer, maintaining the heat until all the ingredients are tender.

Meanwhile, sauté the onion in half of the olive oil in a frying pan/skillet until transparent. Add the pimentón (just for a few seconds, otherwise it will burn) and then the tomatoes. Use a slotted spoon to remove the tomatoes and onions and set aside.

In the same pan, heat the rest of the oil and fry the slice of bread, garlic and almonds. Break the bread into pieces once fried and set aside.

Using a pestle and mortar, pound the fried bread, garlic and almonds to a fine paste. Add the saffron and vinegar and blend with the almond paste. Once the chickpeas are tender, mix in the almond paste and return the onions and tomatoes to the mixture and gently heat through. Season to taste with salt and pepper and serve hot with bread.

'Alboronía' Mozárabe

A PLATE OF MOZARABIC VEGETABLES KNOWN AS 'ALBORONÍA'

Vegetable dishes appear all the time in both home and restaurant cooking and can be enjoyed by themselves or can be accompanied by egg, meat or fish dishes. All over Spain similar recipes are known as '*Pisto*' but in Andalucía it takes its Mozarabic name, '*Alboronía*' or '*Boronía*'. I love it served in a *cazuelita* (small earthenware dish) with some eggs broken on top, gently cooked, leaving the yolks still runny. At home I often serve it on small toasts with a fried quail egg and plenty of freshly ground black pepper on top, together with a little of the flavoursome oil reserved from cooking the vegetables.

1 white onion, peeled and diced
1 courgette/zucchini, peeled
¼ of a butternut squash, peeled
1 green (bell) pepper, deseeded
1 medium aubergine/eggplant
2–3 good-sized tomatoes
50 ml/3½ tablespoons Spanish olive oil
2 teaspoons *pimentón dulce* (Spanish sweet paprika)
sea salt
pine nuts, to garnish

SERVES 4-6

Cut all the vegetables into small cubes. Sprinkle with salt.

Heat the oil in a frying pan/skillet and add all the prepared ingredients, except the pimentón and pine nuts. Cook gently for about 40 minutes, stirring frequently but try not to break their shapes. Push the vegetables to one side of the pan and add the pimentón, cooking it for a few seconds in some of the oil and vegetable juices. Stir into the other ingredients, then transfer to a serving dish.

In a small dry frying pan/skillet, toast the pine nuts until they take a light colour and sprinkle on top of the dish. Serve with fried potatoes cut into squares on the side, if liked.

Flores de alcachofa con jamón Ibérico
FRESH ARTICHOKE FLOWERS WITH IBÉRICO HAM

In Sevilla, modern chefs are creating new recipes that quickly become very popular. Such is the case with these artichoke flowers that I tasted in a small tapas bar in the heart of the city in the popular Barrio de Santa Cruz, close to the magnificent Gothic cathedral. (*Pictured on page 81.*)

freshly squeezed juice of ½ a lemon
a few sprigs of fresh parsley, roughly
    chopped
12 medium round artichokes, peeled
    (they should be very firm inside)
500 ml/2 cups Spanish extra virgin
    olive oil, plus extra for frying
sea salt
8 thin slices of Ibérico ham
Salsa Mahonesa (see page 41), to serve

SERVES 6

Fill a bowl with plenty of water and add the lemon juice and parsley.

Remove the outer green leaves from the artichokes and use a paring knife to cut the top third of each one to reveal the heart. Cut away the stalks and place the artichokes one by one in the bowl of water to prevent the artichokes darkening. .

Drain the artichokes and place them in a saucepan. Cover with the olive oil and add a little salt. Cook over a medium heat for about 30 minutes or until tender. Remove from the pan and leave to cool. With your fingers, carefully open each artichoke.

Heat 2–3 tablespoons olive oil in a large pan. Fry the artichokes upside down until they take some colour and become crunchy. Serve with the ham on top and some Salsa Mahonesa on the side.

Tostada de queso Payoyo, espárragos y miel
ASPARAGUS, PAYOYO CHEESE & HONEY ON RUSTIC BREAD

It was in Cádiz during Carnival a couple of years ago where I discovered Payoyo in the magnificent old market where a local producer was giving a true masterclass. Payoyo is a beautiful and distinctive cheese produced in the Sierra de Grazalema, about an hour or so away from Cádiz city. This tasty cheese made with goat's milk or sheep's milk (or on occasion with both) combines beautifully with asparagus.

20 green asparagus spears
5 slices of rustic bread, lightly toasted
150 g/5½ oz. Payoyo cheese, grated
runny honey, for drizzling
Spanish olive oil, for frying

SERVES 4

Grill the asparagus spears in a cast-iron griddle or frying pan/skillet with a little olive oil until cooked, but still retaining a bite – they should be crunchy.

Place the asparagus on top of the toasts. Sprinkle with grated Payoyo cheese and place under a hot preheated grill/broiler until the cheese starts melting and taking colour.

Remove from under the grill/broiler and serve piping hot, drizzled with honey.

Remojón

ORANGE, COD, ONION & OLIVE SALAD

This is a traditional salad from the province of Granada or even more precisely from the Valle de la Alegría, also known as the Valle de Lecrín. It is a beautiful fertile valley that was chosen in the 10th century by the Arabs to live in and to cultivate oranges, initially bitter oranges, as well as a wide range of fresh vegetables and extensive olive groves. Sweet oranges had to wait until the 18th century to be cultivated in Spain. With some slight variations, Remojón is also prepared in the provinces of Málaga and Almería.

200 g/7 oz. *bacalao* (salted cod)

2 sweet oranges

½ medium white onion or large spring onion/scallion (cebolleta), finely sliced

60 g/½ cup marinated black olives

2 hard-boiled/cooked eggs, peeled and quartered

fresh basil leaves, to garnish

sea alt and freshly ground black pepper, to season

FOR THE DRESSING

2 garlic cloves, left whole

2 tablespoons wine vinegar or 1 tablespoon sherry vinegar

5 tablespoons Spanish extra virgin olive oil

½ teaspoon *pimentón dulce* (Spanish sweet paprika) or freshly ground black pepper, as preferred

SERVES 4

One of the traditional ways to desalinate salted cod is to place it on a hot griddle/grill pan to take some colour, turning once, then transfer it to a bowl and soak it in plenty of water. While in the water, crumble the cod into small portions with your fingers. Leave the cod to soak in the water for 2–3 hours, making certain that it retains some of the salt. Drain and pat dry.

Peel the oranges, remove the pith and slice them into thick rounds or wedges. Place in a serving dish, with the onions and olives.

Toast the garlic cloves for the dressing in a dry frying pan/skillet, then peel and chop the cloves. Mix the garlic, vinegar and olive oil in a small bowl, adding a touch of pimentón (or freshly ground black pepper, if preferred).

Pour the dressing over the salad and stir carefully. Add the eggs and garnish with a few small basil leaves on top before serving.

Guisantes y setas salteadas con panceta de Ibérico
SAUTÉED FRESH PEAS, IBÉRICO PANCETA & WILD MUSHROOMS

This recipe is an ode to probably the most beautiful time of the year, very early spring. This is not a vegetarian dish as it is cooked with *panceta* cured during the winter months in Jabugo, or Cumbres Mayores. I prefer to buy young peas in the pod although it is easy to buy them shelled in local markets. This dish is served as a first course.

125 g/4½ oz. Ibérico panceta, sliced
4 tablespoons Spanish olive oil
150 g/1½ cups wild mushrooms, cleaned
   with a damp cloth, chopped
1 white onion, finely chopped
100 ml/scant ½ cup dry white wine
200 ml/scant 1 cup vegetable stock
750 g/5 cups fresh peas (or frozen peas,
   thawed)
sea salt and freshly ground black pepper

SERVES 4

Fry the panceta in a dry frying pan/skillet over a medium heat until crispy. Remove from the pan and set aside.

Heat 2 tablespoons of the olive oil in the same pan. Add the mushrooms, season and sauté until tender. Remove the mushrooms and set aside.

In the same pan again, heat the remaining olive oil, add the onion and sauté until transparent and very tender. Don't let it take colour.

Pour the wine into the pan and cook until reduced by half. Pour in the vegetable stock, bring it to the boil before adding the peas. Cook the peas until all the liquid has evaporated and the peas are tender.

Return the mushrooms to the pan and stir through. Just before serving, add the pancetta to heat through.

Huevos rotos con patatas fritas y jamón Serrano
BROKEN EGGS WITH FRIED POTATOES & IBÉRICO HAM

Eggs simply fried in plenty of olive oil can be addictive, but when eaten with potatoes and Serrano ham as here, the dish transforms what could be just a basic 'egg and chips' into something magical.

4–5 large new potatoes, peeled and
   sliced
4 thin slices of Serrano ham
4 very fresh large/US extra-large eggs
Spanish extra virgin olive oil, for frying
sea salt

SERVES 4

Salt the potatoes and fry them in a shallow frying pan/skillet in plenty of olive oil. I recommend you to do this in two batches. Fry first over a medium heat and as the potatoes become tender, increase the temperature to make them crispy and golden. Set aside in a warm serving dish with the ham laid on top.

Use the same pan to fry the eggs. You may need to add more oil. Increase the heat and just before it reaches smoking point, add the eggs, one by one. Using a spoon, start pouring hot oil over the yolks to cover them with the thinnest layer of white. Their bottoms will become crispy and lacey.

Lay the crispy eggs on top of the potatoes and Serrano ham – the ham's tasty fat will already be melting over the potatoes. Place the dish on the table and using two knives break the eggs. The yolks will start running over the potatoes and the ham in front of the hungry diners already waiting, bread in hand.

Habitas confitadas con ajos, limón y menta
CONFIT OF BABY BROAD BEANS WITH LEMON, GARLIC & MINT

Fresh baby broad/fava beans just picked from the plant are delicious, especially in a good salad, but they can also be very tasty cooked at a low temperature in olive oil with a small piece of lemon peel, garlic and fresh mint. Small artichokes can also be prepared the same way. This is a lovely dish to accompany other salads, mixed in with scrambled eggs or served with fried eggs. *(Pictured on page 88.)*

400 g/3⅓ cups fresh baby broad/fava
   beans, shelled
a small piece of lemon peel without pith
3 garlic cloves, peeled
a few whole black peppercorns
300 ml/1¼ cups Spanish olive oil
a few sprigs of fresh mint
sea salt

SERVES 2–3

Place a few small mint leaves in a dish of iced water and set aside. These will be used to garnish.

Place the shelled broad/fava beans, lemon peel, garlic, peppercorns and a pinch of salt in a saucepan and cover completely with the oil. Cook at a very low temperature for about 20 minutes. Add the mint sprigs and cook for a further 25 minutes, or until the beans are tender. Set aside and let them cool down in the oil.

Drain the beans, remove and discard the lemon peel, garlic, peppercorns and mint sprigs. Serve with the reserved mint leaves on top to garnish.

Sarten de pimientos rojos asados
ROASTED & SAUTÉED RED PEPPERS

Spanish large red (bell) peppers are available all seasons of the year. Roasted and then sautéed, peppers are included in numerous Spanish recipes. They are so often present in Andalucian cooking that it is worth cooking them in large batches to keep in the fridge, preserved by their own juices and some olive oil. These peppers go very well with cheese, especially plated with a soft Andalucian goat's cheese, and seared slightly with a chef's blow torch. *(Pictured on page 89.)*

2 long sweet red peppers, such as
   Romano or Marconi, left whole
2 tablespoons Spanish extra virgin
   olive oil, plus extra for coating
2–3 garlic cloves, peeled and sliced
sea salt

SERVES 2

Preheat the oven to 180°C/160°C fan/350°F/ Gas 4.

Using your hands, coat the peppers with the oil. Roast on a baking sheet in the preheated oven for 30–35 minutes, turning several times, until the skin becomes translucent, with some black dots of char appearing. Set aside. When warm, peel the peppers, remove the seeds and the skin. Set aside, reserve all the pan juices. Season with salt.

Heat 2 tablespoons olive oil in a cast-iron frying pan/ skillet or any frying pan. Add the garlic and as soon as it takes a little colour, add the peppers and sauté for a couple of minutes. Add the reserved pepper juices and cook for another minute, remove the garlic and serve or bottle for another time, as required.

Ensalada templada de zanahoria, especias y menta

WARM SPICY CARROT SALAD WITH MINT

In the cosmopolitan city of Granada with a student population that exceeds the 65,000 mark, as well as thousands of visitors coming to see the Alhambra each year, it is easy to find delicious food connected with North Africa and the Middle East. This salad is a good example of the fashionable *Cocina Andalusí*. In summer I serve this dish with a plate of Huevos con Salsa Mahonesa y Bonito (see page 41) as well as with grilled asparagus. *(Pictured on page 88–89.)*

a handful of fresh mint leaves
5 large carrots, washed
1 teaspoon cumin seeds
1 teaspoon coriander seeds
3 tablespoons Spanish extra virgin olive oil
½ teaspoon dried chilli/hot red pepper flakes
½ teaspoon ground turmeric
sea salt and freshly ground black pepper, to season

FOR THE PX SHERRY REDUCTION
1 tablespoon PX (Pedro Ximénez) sherry
1 teaspoon sherry vinegar

SERVES 4

To make the PX Sherry Reduction, pour the PX sherry and sherry vinegar into a small saucepan and heat over a medium heat for about 2 minutes until reduced slightly, then set aside until required.

Prepare a large bowl with plenty of iced water and fresh mint leaves and set aside.

Using a potato peeler cut the thinnest and longest of carrot slices you can manage. Place in the iced water for about 15 minutes. Drain, pat dry and season with salt. Place in a serving dish, sprinkle over a few drops of the PX Sherry Reduction, and set aside.

Grind the cumin and coriander seeds using a pestle and mortar.

Just before serving, heat the olive oil in a frying pan/skillet and when hot, add the ground cumin and coriander, cook for a few seconds before adding the chilli/hot red pepper flakes and the turmeric. Be very careful to avoid them burning. Pour the spiced oil over the carrots and serve the salad while still warm.

Potaje de garbanzos con espinacas
CHICKPEA & SPINACH STEW

There are many recipes with chickpeas/garbanzo beans cooked throughout Andalucía and cooks know very well when the perfect time of the year is to buy them. Chickpeas can be small or slightly bigger, of a lighter or darker colour and they can be purchased in glass jars ready to be cooked, but one thing is certain for this particular recipe, they should be bought dried and need to be soaked overnight.

This is a very simple yet hearty and flavoursome vegetarian recipe, perfect to eat on one of those rainy days in winter, with good bread and a glass of a hearty red wine from Ronda. The combination of chickpeas and fresh spinach, together with garlic and onion, cumin and pimentón, bay leaf and tomatoes has never let down any cook, as long as the chickpeas have been cooked properly and they are from the most recent crop if possible.

400 g/2⅓ cups dried chickpeas/
  garbanzo beans
1 bay leaf
50 ml/scant ¼ cup Spanish olive oil
1 onion, finely chopped
1 garlic clove, chopped
2 tomatoes, peeled and chopped
1 teaspoon cumin seeds, ground
  using a pestle and mortar
1 teaspoon *pimentón dulce*
  (Spanish sweet paprika)
350 g/12½ oz. fresh spinach,
  washed and stems picked
1 hard-boiled/cooked egg, peeled
  and chopped
sea salt and freshly ground black
  pepper, to season

SERVES 6

Place the chickpeas/garbanzo beans in a large saucepan, cover with plenty of water and a pinch of salt and leave to soak overnight.

The following morning sieve/strain and wash the chickpeas under running water. Return to the pan, adding fresh water to cover – about 3–4 fingers above the chickpeas. Bring to the boil, then reduce the heat, add the bay leaf and cover with a lid. To become tender, chickpeas need to be cooked at least for 1 hour or even more.

Heat the olive oil in a frying pan/skillet. Add the onion and the garlic and cook until the onion becomes transparent and soft before adding the tomatoes. Bring to the boil and reduce the heat to a moderate temperature, stirring from time to time with a wooden spoon until small oil bubbles appear on the surface of the onion, garlic and tomato mixture (sofrito). Add the cumin, pimentón and some black pepper, stirring to avoid burning the pimentón. Cook for another 1–2 minutes, then set aside.

Once the chickpeas/garbanzo beans are tender, add the sofrito and cook all together for another 30 minutes. If needed add some warm water to loosen (never cold).

Place the spinach in another saucepan, season with a little salt, pour some boiling water over and cook until tender. Strain and squeeze to remove as much water as possible. Add the spinach to the chickpeas, stir and let simmer all together for a couple of minutes.

Place in a serving dish with the chopped egg scattered over the top and serve while hot.

FROM THE FISHMONGER

The Andalucian Fish Counter

When I first started travelling in Andalucía back in the 1980s, I realized how little recognition had been given to the richness and variety of the most extensive land in the whole of Spain, both in terms of agriculture and fisheries and in the amount of quite distinctive dishes found everywhere. In a government publication describing the main characteristics of *Las Cocinas de España* (the cooking of Spain), Spain had been divided from north to south into culinary regions. The Basque Country was associated with sauces (*cocina de las salsas*), Castile with roasted meats (*cocina de los asados*), Valencia with rice dishes (*los arroces*) and Andalucía with fried fish (*pescaíto frito*). Looking back through this publication and thinking about Andalucía, yes it was a very limited description of '*la gastronomía Andaluza*' but it was not wrong, Andalucians so love fried fish, and fry it with great panache. Saying that, the range of seafood dishes of the *Cocina Andaluza* does not begin and end with fried fish and is incredibly extensive and greatly valued by locals and visitors alike.

Of the eight provinces of Andalucía, two enjoy the waters of the Atlantic Ocean (Huelva and Cádiz) and another three (Málaga, Granada and Almería) those of

the warmer Mediterranean Sea. Here local fishermen have been catching fish since the beginning of time and salt harvested from the sea has always been available to preserve it. Andalucía is a major producer of sea salt. In the *Salinas* (salt pans) huge shiny mountains of the whitest salt can be seen near San Fernando in Cádiz and in Huelva. Some of the fish are sold fresh, others are converted as *salazones* (fish cured in salt). Many of these fish which are cured in salt reach higher prices in the market such as the expensive roe (*huevas*) and particularly the true speciality *mojama*, small fillets of salt-cured wild red tuna. Recently in a lovely small bar in Almería I tasted a salad of ripe tomatoes, the sweetest green olives, gherkins (*pepinillos en vinagre*) and the most delicate silver-skinned, slightly salted *bonito* tuna which had been cured by the father of the bar's owner; it was an experience not to be missed.

In Andalucía, a great variety of fresh fish and shellfish dishes can be found, not only in coastal areas, but everywhere, cooked at home or in bars and restaurants. This is nothing new but it has been helped by modern distribution and the presence in cities and

small towns of large retailers. These retailers are encouraged, by popular demand, to have large attractive displays of whole fresh fish and shellfish instead of those that have already been gutted, filleted and packed up in plastic. To do the job properly, trained staff, are contracted to be able to clean and sell fresh fish in store, and yet they still cannot compete with the independent fishmonger, and I rather hope it will remain this way for a while yet. When fishmongers can be found, they continue to sell and supply seafood to their customers and also to restaurants, bringing the catch up every day from the coast, mainly fished in local waters. Where we are in Aracena there are two fishmongers selling from their own shops, fish landed that same morning at local ports in Huelva or Cádiz provinces. They have to compete with two main retailers, one German, the other Spanish, bringing fish every day from their own depots, caught mostly from different waters around the world. Some people, searching for top quality and diversity, prefer to buy fish brought in from small more local ports like La Linea, Barbate or Sanlúcar de Barrameda. These people, increasing now in number have made possible the survival of Luis and Jesús, our local fishmongers. If you need something special they will bring it in themselves as soon as available from the 'lonja', the official wholesalers market at the local

port, at a cost of course. There are the exquisite *gambas blancas* (white prawns/shrimp) from Huelva, the large prawns known as langostinos from Sanlúcar de Barrameda which have the most brilliant texture, the minute *quisquillas* needed to make the *Tortillitas de Camarones de Cádiz* (see page 30), the sardines which the people from Málaga cook to perfection and the *boquerones*, anchovies to cure with vinegar, garlic and olive oil. There are also the medium-sized mackerels always available fresh, the large and small *chocos* (cuttle fish); the *merluza* (hake) to fry 'a la Andaluza'; the large bream family such as the *dorada*; the urta (also known as *parga*) to cook 'a la sal' or 'a la Roteña' (baked with vegetables). Going even further, the food culture of Andalucía is associated with the rich red wild tuna full of special tasty healthy fat, which pass through the Straits of Gibraltar in early May.

In the whole of Spain, but particularly in Andalucía, there is a clear distinction between what they call blue fish (*pescado azul*) and white fish (*pescado blanco*). Until fairly recently, oily blue fish, which includes tuna, mackerel and anchovies, were associated with the lower classes and lower middle class. However this has now changed helped by chefs who are including them on their menus and in amazing recipes such as the Ventresca of Red Tuna with Orange Sauce I have included on page 105.

Gazpachuelo Malagueño
GAZPACHUELO FROM MÁLAGA

There are a number of recipes prepared in Andalucía using the name 'gazpacho'. They may be made with different ingredients, originate from different localities, some served cold (see *Gazpacho Andaluz*, page 64) and some hot, but it was in Málaga some years ago where I discovered *Gazpachuelo* – a rather unusual preparation that intrigued me. So far I have not been able to find out why it is called this but I will keep on trying. It is different from the rest of the gazpachos I know with, something in between a soup and a light stew with a delicate taste.

250 g/9 oz. raw prawns/jumbo shrimp
250 g/9 oz. hake fillet or similar firm white fish, skin on
3 potatoes, peeled and cubed
2 eggs, boiled for 10 minutes, cooled, peeled and grated
Salsa Mahonesa (see page 41)
sea salt and freshly ground black pepper, to season
freshly chopped parsley, to serve

SERVES 4

Bring 1 litre/4 cups salted water to the boil in a large saucepan. Boil the prawns/shrimp until they change colour. Use a slotted spoon to remove them from the water and set aside to cool.

In the same water (now a light stock) poach the hake for 3-4 minutes, or until opaque. Use a slotted spoon to remove the fish from the water and set aside to cool.

Peel the prawns and place in a bowl. Remove the skin of the hake, then flake the fish into the same bowl.

Pour another 1 litre/4 cups water into the saucepan and add the potatoes and some salt. Bring to the boil and cook for about 20 minutes until tender. Drain and set aside.

Add the grated eggs to the bowl with the prawns and hake.

Just before serving, reheat the stock and start pouring in the Salsa Mahonesa stirring constantly, to avoid splitting the emulsion.

Add the potatoes and the seafood mixture and stir through the soup. Adjust the salt to taste and grind some black pepper on top. Garnish with parsley and serve warm.

Mejillones con peladura de limón, cebolla y vino blanco
FRESH MUSSELS WITH LEMON ZEST, ONION & WHITE WINE

Fresh mussels are available all year round, but from September to April they are at their best. This is the time when I love to prepare this easy and original recipe. I tasted it for the first time in a small bar in the old district of El Albaicín, the old Moorish quarter in the city of Granada, just facing The Alhambra.

1.5 kg/3¼ lb. fresh mussels
3 tablespoons Spanish olive oil
1 white onion, peeled and thinly sliced
grated zest of 1 lemon
2 garlic cloves, chopped
200 ml/scant 1 cup dry white wine

SERVES 4

Clean the mussels under cold, running water. Pull off the beards and remove any broken ones.

Heat the oil in a large deep-sided saucepan. Sauté the onion until soft but still white. Add the garlic followed by the lemon zest. Cook for 2 minutes more, add the mussels, stir and pour in the wine, turning the heat right up and covering the pan tightly.

Cook for 2–3 minutes more or until the mussels are open, shaking the pan a couple of times. The mussels should be plump and opaque – don't overcook them or they will shrivel.

Serve with the broth in which they have been cooked, discarding any mussels that have not opened.

Crema de mariscos
CREAM OF SHELLFISH

This light cream of mussels, clams and prawns/ shrimp, makes an elegant and delicate first course.

350 g/12½ oz. fresh mussels, washed
200 g/7 oz. clams, washed
450 g/1 lb. fresh prawns/ shrimp (250 g/9 oz. kept whole, and the heads and shells separated for the rest)
60 ml/¼ cup white wine
100 g/1 stick butter

½ tablespoon plain/ all-purpose flour
250 ml/1 cup whole/ full-fat milk
sea salt

TO SERVE
freshly chopped parsley
freshly chopped dill (optional)

SERVES 4–6

Place the mussels, clams, whole prawns/shrimp and the heads and shells (reserving the peeled prawns) in a large pan. Add 1 litre/4 cups water and the wine and bring to the boil. Reduce the heat and simmer for 2–3 minutes until the clams and the mussels have opened and the prawns have changed colour. Strain and reserve the stock. Remove the shells from the mussels and clams and peel the whole prawns.

In the same pan, melt the butter. Add the flour and cook for a few minutes, stirring. Start adding the reserved stock, stirring to avoid lumps, before adding the milk. Cook for a few minutes until fully integrated. Add the fresh prawns and cook for 2 minutes.

Use a hand-held blender to blend three-quarters of the mussels and half the clams and prawns in a bowl, adding a little stock if needed to loosen. Add this to the creamy stock, adding the reserved prawns. Cook for a couple of minutes, then add the rest of the mussels and clams. Taste and adjust the seasoning. Sprinkle with chopped parsley and dill to serve.

Salpicón de rape y marisco
MONKFISH & SHELLFISH SALAD

Andalucía is a perfect place to prepare dishes such as '*salpicón*', a name that in Medieval Spain was associated with meat. This recipe, which I often serve during the summer months, has its origins across the Atlantic, in Venezuela. Spoilt by the amazing selection of fish and shellfish, as well as the range of summer vegetables very often grown by our friends in the Sierras, I prepare *salpicón* my own way, adding a vinaigrette made with sherry vinegar and olive oil instead of a lemon or lime juice dressing as used in South America. *(Pictured on page 104.)*

8 large raw prawns/shrimp (langostinos), in their shells
1 monkfish tail (about 250 g/9 oz.)
freshly squeezed juice of ½ a small lemon
250 g/9 oz. octopus, boiled and sliced (not too thinly)
1 red (bell) pepper, deseeded and chopped
1 green (bell) pepper, deseeded and chopped
1 large spring onion/scallion (cebollita), white part only, chopped
2 garlic cloves, finely chopped
6–7 cherry tomatoes, halved
2–3 tablespoons Spanish extra virgin olive oil, plus extra for curing
1 tablespoon sherry vinegar
sea salt and freshly ground black pepper, to season
Salsa Mahonesa (see page 41), to serve

SERVES 4

Fill a large bowl with iced water.

In a large saucepan, bring plenty of water to the boil. Add the prawns/shrimp and as soon as they turn red in colour, place them in the iced water until they become very cold. Drain. Remove the heads and shells (they will make the most wonderful stock) and set aside.

Ask the fishmonger to clean the monkfish tail and remove the central bone. You will have two excellent fillets. Slice each fillet but not too thinly. Place the monkfish slices in a bowl with some lemon juice, olive oil and a little salt. Leave it to cure for 1 hour.

Place the prawns, monkfish, octopus and vegetables in a serving dish. Blend the olive oil, sherry vinegar and a little salt in a small bowl and pour over the salad. My family loves to add some homemade Salsa Mahonesa, which I place at the centre of the table for them to serve themselves.

NOTE *These days I buy tender octopus legs from the fishmongers already boiled – it takes too long to prepare it at home. You can substitute the octopus for squid, which you will need to boil yourself.*

Ventresca de atún rojo con salsa de naranja
VESTRESCA OF RED TUNA WITH ORANGE SAUCE

Late April in Andalucía is the perfect time to prepare this recipe. Some of the sweeter oranges are still on the trees and even more importantly, large tunas are swimming through the Straits of Gibraltar on their way to the Mediterranean. In Barbate chefs and home cooks are waiting impatiently for the 'almadraba' boats to return to port. The *almadraba* is an ancient system of nets which is still in use in Andalucía and in the Spanish Levante.

This is a traditional recipe but the sauce is my own idea, inspired by the originality and the quality of the ingredients I bought in Barbate's Mercado de Abastos. In April–May the rich fat of the *ventresca* (tuna belly) works wonderfully with the acidity of orange, but it will taste good any time of the year. *(Pictured on page 107.)*

500-g/1 lb. 2-oz. ventresca of
   red tuna, cut into quarters
Spanish olive oil, for frying
orange slices, to serve
1 tablespoon coarsely ground
   almonds, lightly toasted
   (you will need 1 tablespoon more
   for the sauce so prepare a batch)

FOR THE ORANGE SAUCE
½ teaspoon PX Sherry Reduction
   (see page 87)
1 tablespoon coarsely ground
   almonds, lightly toasted
freshly squeezed juice of 2 large
   oranges
freshly squeezed juice of ½ a lemon
1 teaspoon bitter orange marmalade

SERVES 4

To prepare the Orange Sauce, place the toasted ground almonds in an electric blender together with the rest of the sauce ingredients and blend to combine. When ready, transfer the mixture to a small saucepan and reduce the sauce by one third by simmering it over a medium heat.

Oil a frying pan/skillet with just a few drops of olive oil. When hot add the tuna pieces to the pan and pan-fry them '*al punto*' for 1–2 minutes on each side i.e. just sufficiently for the centre to be just cooked.

Serve individually plated with some Orange Sauce spooned over and around, with slices of orange and the toasted almonds scattered over the top.

Ensaladilla Rusa Malagueña
RUSSIAN SALAD MALAGA-STYLE

All over Andalucía, and in Málaga in particular, the appearance of modern versions of traditional dishes has been inspired not only by renowned chefs believing in innovation and creativity, but also many other cooks working in local restaurants and bars. They are now all prepared to offer their customers plates that just five years ago would have been unthinkable! Their *Ensaladillas Rusas* are a perfect example of this. This is a slightly complex recipe inspired by the amazing one I enjoyed at the restaurant *Chinchin Puerto* in Málaga, but it is worth the trouble.

500 g/1 lb. 2 oz. potatoes, unpeeled, boiled, skinned and diced
1 large carrot, peeled, boiled and diced
½ white onion, finely chopped
2 eggs, boiled for 10 minutes, cooled, peeled and grated
sea salt

FOR THE PRAWN/SHRIMP OIL
300 g/10½ oz. fresh prawns/shrimp, peeled and heads and shells separated (reserving the peeled prawns in the fridge)
200 ml/scant 1 cup sunflower oil

FOR THE PRAWN OIL MAHONESA
2 egg yolks
a pinch of coarse sea salt
freshly squeezed lemon juice or white wine vinegar, to taste
120 ml/½ cup prawn/shrimp oil (see above)
40 ml/scant ¼ cup mild-flavoured Spanish olive oil

SERVES 4

Prepare the prawn/shrimp oil 8 hours in advance, or even better, the day before. To do this, sauté the prawn heads and shells in a couple of tablespoons of the oil until they take a reddish golden colour. Cover with the rest of the sunflower oil. Let it simmer at a low temperature for at least 4 hours. Once cold keep in the fridge to rest for another 4 hours or overnight. Before using, strain the oil through a very fine-mesh sieve/strainer. Do this a couple of times or until the oil is completely clear.

Ensure all the Prawn Oil Mahonesa ingredients are at room temperature. Add the egg yolks, a little coarse sea salt and few drops of lemon juice to a large bowl. With a metal hand whisk, start beating the egg yolks as fast as possible, then start adding the prawn oil, little by little. Beat again and repeat the same many times until practically all the prawn oil has been absorbed (reserving a couple of tablespoons of the prawn oil to be used later). Then start adding the olive oil in the same way. At the end you will have a fairly thick emulsion. Add a few drops of water and whisk again; the mahonesa will become a little thinner and slightly whiter. Add the lemon juice or vinegar to taste and adjust the seasoning if needed. Set aside.

Place the potatoes, carrots, onion and half of the grated egg in a large bowl and check the seasoning. Add a couple tablespoons of the prawn oil mahonesa and blend again using a spatula. Transfer to a serving dish. Spoon a generous layer of mahonesa on top.

Heat a couple of tablespoons of the reserved prawn oil in a frying pan/skillet and sauté the reserved prawns for 2 minutes, turning once. Place them on top of the ensaladilla with a little more grated egg yolk and a few drops of the prawn oil from the pan. Serve immediately.

NOTE *As the oil needs to be poured in very small quantities, use a small jug/pitcher (my mother used to use an egg shell).*

Filetes de salmonete a la vinagreta de hierbabuena
RED MULLET WITH FRESH MINT & A MINT VINAIGRETTE

This is a perfectly elegant dish to serve at a dinner party. I suggest you ask your fishmonger to fillet the red mullet for you. (*Pictured on page 113.*)

leaves from a bunch of fresh mint
freshly squeezed lemon juice, to taste
150 ml/⅔ cup Spanish extra virgin
   olive oil
6 large red mullet, filleted and
   pin-boned
2 tablespoons unsalted very soft butter
fine sea salt and ground white pepper

SERVES 6

Preheat the oven to 200°C/180°F fan/400°F/ Gas 4.

First prepare the vinaigrette. In a bowl, using a hand whisk, blend a few finely chopped mint leaves with some lemon juice and olive oil. Season to taste with salt and white pepper then set aside.

Make 2 deep cuts in the side of the fish skin, taking care not to cut all the way through. Season with salt and white pepper. Insert 2 whole mint leaves in each cut and brush with a little butter and a little water.

Place the fish, skin-side up, in a greased ovenproof dish. Cover with foil and bake in the preheated oven for about 6–7 minutes. Remove from the oven and leave to cool down slightly.

Serve each fillet with the vinaigrette spooned on top and around.

Bonito 'en escabeche'
WHITE TUNA 'ESCABECHE'

'Escabeche' is a method of preserving fish or meat in oil and vinegar that has existed in Spain since time immemorial. Today, tuna is prepared by home cooks and chefs, or bought already preserved in cans or jars.

500 ml/2 cups Spanish olive oil
1 large white onion, thinly sliced
6 garlic cloves, peeled
500-g/1 lb. 2-oz. fresh tuna loin
   in one piece
8 sprigs of fresh parsley
6–7 sprigs of fresh thyme
5 tablespoons sherry vinegar
5 tablespoons white wine vinegar
600 ml/2½ cups Manzanilla sherry
10 whole black peppercorns
2 teaspoons fine sea salt

SERVES 6 AS AN APPETIZER

Heat 2 tablespoons of the olive oil in a large saucepan. Sauté the onion and garlic until translucent and tender. Do not let them take colour.

Place the tuna in the pan and add the herbs, vinegars, sherry, remaining olive oil, peppercorns and salt and top up with enough cold water to cover the tuna completely. Cover and bring to the boil, reduce to a simmer and cook for about 1½ hours until the tuna is very tender. Start checking frequently with a thin skewer after 1 hour of cooking time. You don't to cook it for too long after it has become tender as it will fall apart, and also ensure it is not sticking to the bottom of the pan. Remove from the heat, let cool and leave to marinate in the liquid for at least 24 hours in the fridge.

To serve, cut the tuna into thick slices across the grain, spoon the onion from the bottom of the pan onto the slices and serve at room temperature with Roasted & Sautéed Red Peppers (see page 86).

Arroz 'a la Sevillana' en paella

SEVILLA-STYLE PAELLA

In 1992 I was invited together with a group of food and wine writers to visit the universal exposition (EXPO) in Sevilla. We were offered a tasty *Arroz a la Sevillana*, cooked in front of us in a paella pan. This was not a classic *Paella Valenciana* and it did not feature any of the cooking and ingredient restrictions attached to the Valenciana. It included, among many other ingredients, chorizo, shellfish and fish. It was also quite delicious and very colourful. This is a *seco* (dry) rice dish in style (see page 44).

75 g/2¾ oz. cooking chorizo, sliced
500 g/1 lb. 2 oz. clams, washed under cold running water
1 small onion, chopped
2 garlic cloves, peeled
250 g/9 oz. squid, cleaned and chopped
250 g/9 oz. monkfish, deboned and cut into pieces
150 g/5½ oz. *jamón serrano* (serrano ham), chopped
250 g/1⅔ cups fresh peas
500 g/2⅔ cups Andalucían 'round rice'
a few Spanish saffron filaments
1 tablespoon freshly chopped parsley
Spanish olive oil, for frying
sea salt

TO SERVE
2 hard-boiled/cooked eggs, cooled, peeled and quartered
lemon wedges, for squeezing
2 roasted red (bell) peppers, cut into strips (see page 142), or from a jar

SERVES 6

First sauté the chorizo in a small frying pan/skillet with little olive oil for just a few minutes until the oil has been released and the chorizo is starting to crisp. Set aside.

Place the clams in a saucepan with a little water. Heat and let the clams open. Discard any that have remained closed or have their shells broken. Drain, reserving the clam stock and keeping it warm. Reserve the clams.

Heat 3 tablespoons olive oil in a large shallow saucepan or paella pan. Sauté the onion until golden. Add 1 of the garlic cloves and stir. Add the squid and monkfish and stir well before adding the ham and the peas. Stir again and pour in 1.5 litres/6 cups water. Bring to the boil, then cook until the squid and the rest of the fish are almost tender. Sprinkle the rice around the pan and stir gently for the last time. Add the warm clam stock. Taste and adjust the seasoning.

Using a pestle and mortar, pound the second garlic clove, a few saffron filaments and the chopped parsley to a paste, then add this to the rice and leave to cook, uncovered, for about 18 minutes. Do not stir during this time and do not overcook the rice.

Scatter the chorizo and the clams around the pan and cook for a further 5 minutes to heat through.

When ready to serve, let it rest for a couple of minutes before serving with a few drops of lemon juice, decorate with the eggs and strips of roasted red (bell) pepper.

Calabacines 'marinera'
COURGETTES 'MARINERA'

Courgettes/zucchini are normally included in the baskets brought in summer by our friends in Aracena when coming for lunch or dinner. This recipe can be prepared with all kinds of white fish although I prefer to use hake as it flakes beautifully. This is a type of 'sea and land' Mediterranean-style recipe that also includes vermouth and white wine, which is rather unusual.

4 courgettes/zucchini
500 ml/2 cups Spanish olive oil
450 g/1 lb. large white onions, peeled and thinly sliced
200 g/7 oz. hake fillet, uncooked and flaked
200 g/7 oz. button mushrooms, cleaned and sliced
a pinch of freshly grated nutmeg
25 g/¼ cup dried breadcrumbs
1 medium/US large egg, beaten
175ml/¾ cup white vermouth
350 ml/1½ cups fish stock (see below)
sea salt and freshly ground black pepper, to season

FOR THE FISH STOCK
2 tablespoons Spanish olive oil
½ a white onion in one piece
500 g/1 lb. 2 oz. fish and head bones
125 ml/½ cup dry white wine
a bundle of fresh parsley stalks, a sprig of thyme and a bay leaf tied with a string/twine into a 'bouquet garni'
sea salt

SERVES 4

First make the fish stock. Heat the olive oil in a saucepan over a medium heat and sauté the onion until softened. Add the fish bones, stirring occasionally, and cook for a few minutes. Pour in the white wine and reduce a little before adding 750 ml/3¼ cups water. Drop in the bouquet garni and season with salt. Bring to the boil, then reduce the heat and simmer for about 25 minutes, skimming and discarding the surface debris as needed. Sieve/strain into a bowl and reserve.

Peel the courgettes/zucchini in narrow strips and reserve the skins. Cut each courgette in half lengthways and scoop out the pulp along with the seeds. Save the pulp and seeds and reserve the courgette shells.

Heat half the olive oil in a large frying pan/skillet. Sauté half the onions until transparent before adding the hake, courgette pulp and seeds and the mushrooms. Season with salt and pepper and a touch of nutmeg. Stir and cook for a few minutes. Add the breadcrumbs and the egg and cook at a moderate heat for another 10 minutes. Set aside.

Heat the remaining oil in a saucepan. Sauté the remaining onions until transparent and tender. Add the reserved courgette skins, sauté for a few more minutes before adding the vermouth first and then the fish stock. Cook for a few minutes more, then transfer to a food processor and blend until smooth. Set aside.

Preheat the oven to 165°C/145°C fan/325°F/Gas 3.

Use a spoon to fill the courgette shells with the fish and vegetable mixture. Place in a shallow ovenproof dish and pour over the blended sauce. Bake for about 10 minutes or until the courgettes take a lovely colour. Serve hot.

NOTE *To prepare the fish stock, ask your fishmonger for some bones and head of white fish.*

Lubina 'a la sal'
SEA BASS COOKED IN A SALT CRUST

For those who like perfectly cooked fish, cooking 'a la sal' is an easy technique to master. It guarantees success as the salt surprisingly does not permeate into the fish meat, yet it allows the fish to remain perfectly moist in a unique way, truly a dream of a fish course. It is like cooking 'en papillote' with salt instead of paper.

In Malaga I have eaten delicious lubina (sea bass) cooked in salt then simply brushed with an emulsion of pounded garlic, extra virgin olive oil and a touch of lemon juice with parsley and a Pipirrana de Jaén-style salad (see page 67).

2 kg/4½ lb. coarse sea salt,
   or a little more if needed
1 egg white, lightly beaten
Spanish olive oil, for brushing
1–1.5 kg/1 lb. 2 oz.–3¼ lb. sea bass
   or sea bream (see Note)

SERVES 4

Preheat the oven to 190°C/170°C fan/375°F/Gas 5.

Put the coarse sea salt in a bowl and blend with the beaten egg white.

Line an oven tray with baking paper and brush the paper lightly with olive oil. Place the fish on top and cover completely with the salt and egg mixture, tightening around with your hands. The fish should be completely covered, just leaving the tail uncovered. Using a knife, mark the fish outline and then the outline of the head – this will help remove the crust once cooked. Bake in the preheated oven for about 28–30 minutes. A good trick is to pull the tail and if it comes free easily, the fish is cooked.

Once ready, remove from the oven and using a knife, again mark even further the outline of the body and the head, which will make it easier for the removal of the crust. The fish will appear completely clean without the skin and scales. Then it will be easy to remove the fillets without any salt attached and serve onto individual plates.

NOTE *I recommend you find a fishmonger who can get you a good-size sea bass or whole bream still with its head and scales (the scales will remain attached to the crust while cooking). Also note that the fish must be gutted by making only a very small incision in the belly.*

Urta 'a la Roteña'
ROTA-STYLE BAKED SEA BREAM

Humble in origin, this is a fishermans' dish from the coastal town of Rota in the province of Cádiz. The dish is traditionally prepared with a fish called *urta* (red-banded sea bream). However, if I cannot find this I use a good-size sea bream. In Sanlúcar de Barrameda is the bar and restaurant called *Bigote*, probably the best known in town. Fernando Bigote offers his clients the most fantastic version of this dish. Having started life as a fisherman from an early age, Fernando not only serves the freshest fish, he buys all his vegetables locally, vegetables which are renowned all over the region, including the potatoes. Using ripe tomatoes will make an enormous difference while preparing Andalucian dishes.

1 large whole sea bream (about
    1.5 kg/3½ lb.) or 2 smaller ones
a few drops of freshly squeezed
    lemon juice
2 large potatoes, peeled and sliced
    into thin rounds
2 garlic cloves
1 large white onion, sliced
250 g green (bell) peppers,
    deseeded and chopped
500 g/1 lb. 2 oz. ripe tomatoes,
    blanched, peeled and chopped
125 ml/½ cup Manzanilla sherry
    from Sanlúcar or dry white wine
Spanish extra virgin olive oil
sea salt and freshly ground black
    pepper, to season

SERVES 4

Preheat the oven to 180°C/160°C fan/350°F/Gas 4.

Season the cleaned fish inside and outside with salt and pepper. Blend a little water with a few drops of lemon juice.

Bring the potatoes to the boil in a large saucepan of water and boil for 2–3 minutes. Drain.

Heat a little olive oil in a large ovenproof dish. When hot, add the potatoes and cover with aluminium foil. Place in the preheated oven and bake for about 15 minutes. They should not take colour. Take the potatoes out of the oven, remove the foil and mix the potatoes in with the oil in the bottom of the dish. Place the seasoned fish on top of the potatoes, covering as much of the potatoes as possible. Pour the water and lemon juice mixture over the top. Return to the oven and cook for about 15 minutes. Make certain the fish does not overcook.

While the fish and potatoes are cooking, prepare a sofrito sauce in a pan. Heat 2–3 tablespoons olive oil. When hot, add the onion and cook to soften without taking colour, followed by the green (bell) pepper and the tomatoes. Cook until they become soft, stirring from time to time. Add the wine, bring to the boil and cook for about 15 minutes, until the wine has reduced and a few bubbles of the oil appear on the surface.

Remove the fish and potatoes from the oven. Reduce the oven temperature to 170°C/150°C fan/325°F/Gas 3 and cover with the sofrito *sauce*. Return to the oven and cook for a few minutes more.

To serve, remove the fish from the dish and place on a wooden board. Remove the skin completely and separate the fillets. Plate individually with the potatoes underneath and the fillets of fish on top, covered with some of the sofrito sauce.

Cazuela de fideos con almejas y gambas
'FIDEO' PASTA WITH CLAMS & PRAWNS

Málaga excels in the preparation of seafood they often called 'cazuelas'. Cazuelas are traditional earthenware pots that give their name to dishes, even if today they may not have been prepared in one. *Fideo* is a fine noodle pasta that has been eaten in Spain since its introduction by the Arabs in the Middle Ages.

100 g/3½ oz. *fideo* pasta, medium size or broken *vermicelli*
a few fresh mint leaves, to garnish
sea salt

FOR THE PRAWN/SHRIMP STOCK
300 g/10 oz. fresh large prawn/shrimp heads and shells (reserve the prawns)

FOR THE CLAM JUICE
200 g/7 oz. clams
Spanish olive oil, for sautéing
a splash of white wine
a handful of freshly chopped parsley

FOR THE SOFRITO
40 ml/2½ tablespoons Spanish olive oil
300 g/10 oz. large ripe tomatoes, peeled and roughly grated
1 green (bell) pepper, deseeded and finely chopped
2 garlic cloves, finely chopped
½ teaspoon *pimentón dulce* (Spanish sweet paprika)
a few saffron filaments

SERVES 4

To prepare the prawn/shrimp stock, cover the prawn shells and heads with 800 ml/3½ cups water in a saucepan. Bring to the boil, reduce the heat and simmer for about 10–15 minutes. Discard the shells and keep the stock hot.

To prepare the clam juice, sauté the clams in a small frying pan/skillet in a little olive oil. When the clams start opening add the wine and a little water. Cover and cook for 2–3 minutes or until they have all opened. Drain and blend the prawn stock with the clam juice and keep warm until needed.

For the sofrito, heat the oil in a large frying pan/skillet. Add the grated tomatoes and cook for 5 minutes. Add the green (bell) pepper, cook until almost tender, then add the garlic and stir. Making space in the corner of the pan, sauté the pimentón, stirring to avoid burning, and mix with the tomatoes and green pepper. Add the saffron that has been dissolved in a tablespoon of stock. Continue cooking at a moderate heat, stirring continuously, until all the ingredients are well integrated and quite soft.

Add the hot stock (reserving a little in case it might be needed at the end), stir and cook for a few minutes more. Increase the heat and when it starts bubbling, sprinkle the fideo pasta into the pan. Cook for a few more minutes until they start to soften. Reduce the heat and taste and adjust the seasoning with salt if needed. Add the clams and the reserved prawns and wait until the pasta is cooked a little more than 'al dente'. Don't let the stock be completely absorbed – this is not a completely dry pasta dish. Serve garnished with a few mint leaves on top.

NOTE *To prepare this dish I use a paella pan for six servings or a shallow frying pan/skillet.*

Calamares 'en gabardina'
SQUID IN BEER BATTER

In Andalucía frying is an art, particularly in the city of Sevilla but also in many other places in the region. In Sevilla it is easy to find a *freiduría*, a takeaway shop and restaurant where people will queue to eat fish there or to take home in the classic *cucurucho* (paper cone). Although in the *freidurías* fish is normally fried just coated with a special flour prepared for frying fish (*harina semolosa de trigo*, see page 29), this recipe however really calls for a special coating, a beer batter of a lovely reddish colour known as '*gabardina*' (raincoat). I love to use this beer batter to fry prawns/ shrimp, cuttlefish and squid, as here.

500 g/1 lb. 2 oz. squid, cleaned
   and cut into rings
fine sea salt and ground white
   pepper, to season plain/
   all-purpose flour, for coating
Spanish olive oil, for frying
lemon wedges, for squeezing

FOR THE BEER BATTER
150 g/1 cup plain/all-purpose flour,
   sifted
1 whole medium/US large egg and
   2 egg whites
a few saffron filaments
200 ml/¾ cup beer
2 tablespoons Spanish olive oil

SERVES 4

To prepare the squid, first dry each ring very well (this is very important) and season well with salt and white pepper. Coat lightly with a little flour (this is also very important as without the flour the batter won't stick to the squid properly).

To prepare the beer batter, place the sifted flour in a mixing bowl. Make a hole in the middle of the flour and add the salt, the whole egg and the saffron. Using a fork, break the whole egg and start mixing with the flour. Working with a metal whisk, start pouring in the beer, bit by bit, and work fast until you obtain a creamy batter. Cover with the olive oil and let it rest for at least 30 minutes.

In a separate clean bowl, whisk the egg whites to peaks using an electric hand-held mixer.

Blend the oil into the beer batter and use a spatula to start adding half of the whisked egg whites very carefully, folding from the bottom to the top to avoid losing the air. When integrated, add the rest of the whisked egg whites and work the same way. Set aside.

Heat plenty of oil in an electric fryer or a deep saucepan to a maximum of 170–180°C/320–350°F (use a thermometer if possible). To avoid splattering, check the squid has been properly patted dry before frying.

Place the bowl containing the beer batter close to the fryer. Dip each squid ring in the batter and very carefully drop them into the oil. Almost immediately, they will start puffing up. Turn them over and fry until they they take a reddish colour. Remove the squid rings from the oil and place on kitchen paper. They should be eaten piping hot with a squeeze of lemon juice.

Vieiras salteadas con crema de coliflor y mojo picón

PAN-FRIED SCALLOPS WITH CAULIFLOWER CREAM & SPICY MOJO

Come the summer, family and friends start descending to our home EL Zauzal which is something we all look forward to. This is the time the kitchen truly comes alive, particularly at breakfast time, when each one prepares their own, while the young ones still sleeping will follow. Later some people will go shopping in our nearest town while my daughter-in-law will bake bread or a delicious pie. I normally cook lunch and if we are staying at home in the evening, my son Daniel, who cooks at a professional level, will do the honours. For this recipe, Luis, our local fishmonger, will always be prepared to bring from the coast any fish and shellfish he may not have daily. We all love scallops and this recipe, cooked by Dan with his own *Mojo Picón* sauce recipe too, has become one of the treats of the house.

6 large scallops, corals removed
1 tablespoon sunflower oil
40 g/3 tablespoons butter
finely snipped chives, to serve
sea salt flakes, to serve

FOR THE CAULIFLOWER CREAM
250 g/9 oz. cauliflower, washed and cut into large florets
100 ml/scant ½ cup double/ heavy cream
a dash of white wine vinegar
fine sea salt, to season

FOR DAN'S MOJO PICÓN
½ teaspoon cumin seeds
¼ teaspoon dried chilli/hot red pepper flakes
½ teaspoon *pimentón dulce* (Spanish sweet paprika)
½ teaspoon sea salt flakes
½ teaspoon brown sugar
½ red (bell) pepper, deseeded and very finely diced
1 garlic clove, peeled
a dash of sherry vinegar
200 ml/scant 1 cup Spanish light olive oil or sunflower oil

SERVES 6

To prepare the Cauliflower Cream, boil the cauliflower florets in a saucepan of salted water until very tender, drain well and leave to cool a little. Use a handheld blender or food processor to blend the cauliflower until completely smooth, then add the cream. Continue to blend and add salt and white wine vinegar to taste.

Make the Mojo Picón using a pestle and mortar. Pound the cumin seeds, chilli/hot red pepper flakes, paprika, salt and brown sugar to form a fine powder. Add the garlic and continue to pound until a smooth paste is formed. Add the (bell) pepper and pound again to a final paste. Add the sherry vinegar, then start adding the oil, little by little, to form an emulsion, until all the oil is incorporated.

Season the scallops and dry very well. Add a tablespoon of sunflower oil to a searing hot frying pan/skillet, and place the scallops, flat-side down (scallops have a flat and a more rounded side). After a couple of minutes, turn over, reduce the heat a little and add the butter. A foam should form. Spoon the foam over the scallops while cooking for another minute or so. Remove and place on kitchen paper to drain.

In a serving bowl or plate, place one serving spoon of the cream of cauliflower and place the scallop in the centre of the cream. Spoon a teaspoon of the Mojo Picón on top of each scallop and sprinkle with finely chopped chives and a pinch of sea salt flakes.

NOTE *Any leftover Mojo Picón will keep well in a sealed containter in the fridge for several days.*

THEY ALSO
LOVE MEAT

Meat in Andalucía

During the 1990s, press trips for food writers became a very effective way for Spain to promote its unique and distinctive quality foods and wines. The trips were associated with different areas of production and local gastronomy. Diverse Andalucía, so rich in olives and olive oils, rice, fish and shellfish, charcuterie, fresh meats, fruits and vegetables and, of course, wines, became a perfect destination.

It was when visiting a young olive grove near Córdoba, that I had organized for a group of British journalists, that the great passion in the region for meat became clear to me. During the visit we decided to have dinner in one of the most renowned and traditional restaurants in the city of Córdoba called *El Churrasco* not far from the unbelievably beautiful *mezquita* (cathedral). It was winter, we were cold and the place was not particularly warm. One thing that caught our attention was the lovely green of the tablecloths placed on top of thick overhanging drapes we call *faldas* in Spanish, meaning 'skirts', which were placed over each table. As we sat down, we could not believe our luck. Under the *faldas* the area under the table was heated with a charcoal brazier, well

protected of course, and we could rest our feet on top of a wooden platform above the cold stone floor.

Once settled in, we were served fried aubergines/eggplant with honey, among many other specialities, including thinly sliced cured hams and a variety of cured sausages. On the table appeared a number of salads and a small bowl of *salmorejo* (the local gazpacho) served before the meat course, which we had ordered individually. We could not believe the selection: *Churrasco Cordobés al Carbón de Encina* (pork fillet cooked over charcoal of local holm oak); *Rabo de Toro* (oxtail); *Chuletillas de Cordero* (tender little chops of lamb); *Pierna de Cordero al Horno* (roasted leg of lamb); *Chuleta de Ternera al Carbón* (veal chop cooked on charcoal); *Chuletón de Vacuno* (charcoal-grilled rib of beef); *Parrillada Mixta* (mixed grill) and *Carrilleras en Salsa* (pork cheeks in a sauce). These were all on the menu. Apart from the different cuts and various types of meat our dinner showcased a combination of classic Andalucian recipes and the great love for grilled and barbecued meat specialities. The type of wood charcoal used and preferred by the chef was also distinctive. We also tasted the different

sauces traditionally served with the classic *Churrasco Cordobés*. I need to go back to Córdoba and to El Churrasco, where I am sure nearly all these dishes will still be on the menu – it takes a long time for an Andalucian to change food alliances and traditions, but taking into consideration the creative world of today's Spanish kitchen, I am also sure that the head chef there will be searching for a few more delicious and innovative recipes to cook.

While talking about meat and tastes in a land as large and diverse as Andalucía, it is also important to acknowledge local tastes and customs, particularly variations between inland and coastal localities, as well as those in the high Sierras. A good example is the meat favoured in Aracena by home cooks, and also by professional ones, where little has changed in the last twenty years (or perhaps even in the last few hundred years). Not only for those who could always afford to eat plenty of meat, particularly very expensive cuts, but also for those who could only manage tasty *cocidos* and stews using lesser cuts of meat, such as fresh or cured and salted bones, pulses/legumes and plenty of vegetables that are rarely presented on the menus in local restaurants now. It is interesting that following popular demand and the fact that many women are also out working today, some top restaurants may offer hearty 'homey' dishes that

our mothers and grandmothers would have made and that we all still love, in addition to their lunch menu.

In Andalucía in general, but in western Andalucía in particular, pork occupies a prime position in butchers' shops, sold both as fresh meat and as cured meats. Here, as an alternative to lamb and chicken, fresh pork is regularly used in different cuts sold under interesting names, such as *secreto*, *presa*, *pluma* (all located in different parts of the back, nearer the neck) and *solomillo* (the fillet), among other cuts. Also very popular are the *carrilleras* (pork cheeks) that are cooked in a wonderful stew.

When travelling in the region it is worth visiting local butchers' shops. Aracena, for instance, is a major area of Ibérico pork production with a long history of food preferences, some of which are still not only related to availability, but also to very old religious food customs. Here, butchers' counters are normally divided into four or five sections. A small one for chicken, rabbits and small game, another single one for beef and lamb, then two or three large sections just for pork, and the last one for cured hams and chorizos. Here it is not difficult to imagine which type of meat locals prefer and what to expect when eating in a local restaurant. In a different town on the coast, the meat dishes will be very different as the meat will probably come from other parts of the country.

Paula's arroz con pollo
PAULA'S RICE WITH CHICKEN

This is not a paella. This is a popular Andalucian *Arroz con Pollo*. I have followed the recipe by Paula, the wife of a dear friend Javier Hidalgo (the man behind the success of the beautiful sherry Manzanilla La Gitana, in Sanlúcar de Barrameda, Cádiz). I love to cook this rice as an '*arroz meloso*', which is not completely dry (see page 44).

1 medium chicken, cut into
    6–8 pieces
100 ml/scant ½ cup Spanish
    olive oil
a good splash of Manzanilla sherry
1 white onion, chopped
1 garlic clove, finely chopped
1 red (bell) pepper, deseeded
    and chopped
1 green (bell) pepper, deseeded
    and chopped
2 medium tomatoes, chopped
saffron filaments, to taste, toasted
    in a dry frying pan/skillet and
    dissolved in a little warm stock
250 ml/1 cup chicken stock,
    plus a little more if needed
450 g/2½ cups long-grain rice
sea salt and ground black pepper,
    to season

SERVES 4–6

Season the chicken with salt and pepper. In a deep frying pan/skillet, heat 3 tablespoons of the olive oil. Sauté the chicken pieces until they take some colour. Add the sherry and reduce, then use a slotted spoon to remove the chicken from the pan and set aside.

Add the rest of the oil to the same pan. Add the onion and cook until tender without taking any colour. Add the garlic, followed by the red and green (bell) peppers and cook until almost tender before adding the tomatoes. Cook for a further 5 minutes.

Add the saffron, chicken stock and 750 ml/3¼ cups water. Return the chicken to the pan. Bring to the boil, then reduce the heat and cook uncovered until the chicken is almost tender. Sprinkle the rice on top. Stir only once. Cook for a further 15–18 minutes. The rice should never be overcooked. Leave it to rest for a few more minutes before serving.

Arroz cortigero de las marismas Sevillanas
RICE WITH WILD DUCK 'CORTIGERO STYLE'

This is a full-flavoured *arroz caldoso* (soupy rice) that takes its name from the *cortijos* (country houses) dotted among the marshlands of the Sevilla province. The stock that results from cooking the duck and vegetables imparts a delicious flavour to the rice. In Jerez de la Frontera, the late José Antonio Valdespino prepared this rice to perfection. Traditionally the *arroz cortigero* is prepared in *cazuela* (earthernware dish) but you can use any suitable pot or pan.

1 wild duck, cut into 10 pieces

4–5 tablespoons Spanish extra virgin olive oil

4–5 garlic cloves, peeled

½ a white onion, finely chopped

½ red (bell) pepper, deseeded and cut into squares

1 green (bell) pepper, deseeded and cut into squares

2 large tomatoes, blanched, peeled and chopped

250 g/1⅓ cups Bomba rice or Spanish short-grain rice

sea salt

freshly chopped parsley, to garnish

SERVES 6

Season the duck with salt. In a large round cast-iron pot or similar saucepan, sauté the duck in the olive oil. After a few minutes start turning the pieces of duck until they start taking colour but don't let them dry out.

Add the garlic, onion and peppers and sauté until soft. Add the tomatoes and cook for another 10 minute before adding 2.5 litres/quarts cold water. Bring to the boil, then reduce the heat a little and simmer for about 45 minutes. Don't let the liquid reduce too much as you still need to cook the rice.

By now the water should have become a substantial stock and the duck and vegetables will be quite tender. This is the moment to sprinkle the rice on top. Stir only once. The rice will need about 18 minutes to cook. As this is an '*arroz caldoso*' (soupy rice) you may need to add some extra hot water, but do not stir if possible. When ready, leave it to rest for a few minutes more and serve sprinkled with chopped parsley.

Pinchitos morunos
MOORISH SKEWERS 'ANDALUSÍ'

Al-Andalus was the name given to Spain by the Moors and *Andalusí* is the name given to food with North African flavours prepared in Andalucía. While cooks prefer to use pork or chicken, an authentic recipe calls for lamb with a great combination of spices.

2 tablespoons cumin seeds
2 tablespoons coriander seeds
2 garlic cloves, crushed
1 teaspoon *Pimentón de la Vera*
    (Spanish hot smoked paprika)
2 teaspoons ground turmeric
1 teaspoon ground cinnamon
1 tablespoon dried oregano
100 ml/scant ½ cup Spanish extra
    virgin olive oil
freshly squeezed juice of 1 lemon
1-kg/2¼-lb. leg of lamb, diced
sea salt and freshly ground black
    pepper, to season

MAKES 6-8 SKEWERS

Pound the cumin and coriander seeds using a large pestle and mortar. Next, pound the garlic followed by the rest of the spices and the oregano. Using a spatula, blend it all together. Start pouring in the olive oil, little by little, using the pestle to mix. Add the lemon juice and season with salt and pepper.

With your hands, rub the marinade all over the leg of lamb and leave to marinate, covered, in the fridge overnight.

The following morning, thread the pieces of lamb onto skewers. Cook on a preheated hot barbecue grill 10-15 minutes, taking care to not let the meat dry out. Serve with sautéed or fried potatoes and a simple tomato and onion salad.

Pollo al horno con pasas y piñones
ROAST CHICKEN WITH RAISINS & PINE NUTS

It was on a wine trip to Córdoba, a long time ago, where I encountered this recipe for the first time. It had been cooked for a Sunday dinner by a friend. I loved its simplicity and the complex flavours given by the combination of the dried fruits and the wine.

1.5-kg/3½-lb. whole organic chicken
Spanish extra virgin olive oil, for
    brushing
20 g/1½ tablespoons butter
50 g/⅓ cup raisins or sultanas/golden
    raisins, soaked for 30 minutes
    then drained
50 g/⅓ cup pine nuts
8 tablespoons dry Oloroso sherry
sea salt and freshly ground black
    pepper, to season

SERVES 4-6

Preheat the oven to 180°C/160°C fan/350°F/ Gas 4.

Season the chicken with salt and black pepper and brush with olive oil. Roast in the preheated oven for about 1½ hours until brown, basting occasionally. Transfer to a warmed serving dish or a traditional Spanish earthenware *cazuela*.

Heat the butter in a frying pan/skillet and sauté the raisins and pine nuts. Add to the chicken, pour over the sherry and taking great care, ignite to briefly 'flambé' just before serving. This is good with sautéed or fried potatoes on the side.

Solomillo de cerdo marinado, patatas panaderas y pimientos rojos asados

MARINATED IBÉRICO PORK FILLET, ROAST POTATOES & RED PEPPERS

One of the great things about living in the middle of the Andalucían forest – the *Dehesa* – is to have access to fresh and cured Ibérico pork meat all year round. The Dehesa forest is the natural habitat of the Ibérico breed of pig. Here he roams free, searching for acorns, his favourite food. I think this dish tastes best if the cumin seeds and the peppercorns are pounded using a pestle and mortar but if you already have ground spices, use them instead. Remember to let the meat marinate overnight if possible. *(Pictured on pages 140–141.)*

3 garlic cloves, finely chopped
½ teaspoon sea salt
3 teaspoons cumin seeds
3 teaspoons whole black
   peppercorns
2 teaspoons *pimentón dulce*
   (Spanish sweet paprika)
2 teaspoons dried oregano
50 ml/3½ tablespoons Spanish
   olive oil, plus extra for drizzling
750-g/1 lb.-10 oz. pork fillet,
   trimmed of excess fat
3 red (bell) peppers, left whole,
   rinsed and patted dry
sea salt and freshly ground
   black pepper, to season

FOR THE SLICED POTATOES
350 g/12½ oz. potatoes,
   peeled and thinly sliced
3 tablespoons Spanish olive oil
1 white onion, sliced
1 teaspoon salt

SERVES 6

Pound together the garlic and salt using a mortar and pestle. Add the cumin, black peppercorns and pimentón and pound again. Add the oregano and the oil and mix together. Season the pork, rub the spice mixture all over and leave to marinate, covered, in the fridge overnight.

When you are ready to cook, preheat the oven to 180°C/160°C fan/350°F/Gas 4.

Place the red (bell) peppers in an ovenproof dish and drizzle with some olive oil. Bake in the preheated oven for 30–40 minutes, turning once or twice. When the skin on the peppers has wrinkled, remove from the oven and leave to cool. Remove the seeds and skins, slice thinly and reserve on the oven dish, covered.

To make the potatoes, place the sliced potatoes and onion in an ovenproof tray, season and drizzle with olive oil. Place in the hot oven. When the potatoes have been cooking for about 20 minutes, heat a heavy frying pan/skillet – I use a cast-iron one, large enough to contain all the meat – over a high heat. Brown the pork turning every minute or so for about 5 minutes until it is well browned on all sides. Remove the pork from the pan. Place it on top of the potatoes and cook for a further 20 minutes or a little less if you prefer the meat a little pink at the centre.

Take the pork from the oven and leave it to rest for several minutes. You may need to increase the oven temperature and return the potatoes to the oven to let them take a lovely colour. Warm the red peppers and when ready, slice the pork.

I normally plate this dish with a layer of potatoes, the meat and then the red peppers on top, drizzled with a few drops of the pan juices.

Churrasco de Córdoba con sus salsas
PORK FILLET FROM CÓRDOBA WITH TRADITIONAL SAUCES

In Córdoba this recipe normally calls for pork fillet, but it can also be prepared with well-cured beef. This is a perfect dish to cook in a hot griddle pan or even better let it sizzle on a barbecue in the hot summer months.

500-g/1 lb. 2-oz. pork fillet
　trimmed of excess fat
coarse sea salt, to season

FOR THE RED SAUCE
3 garlic cloves, peeled
½ teaspoon cumin seeds
½ teaspoon cayenne pepper
½ teaspoon *pimentón dulce*
　(Spanish sweet paprika)
200 ml/scant 1 cup Spanish
　extra virgin olive oil
sea salt and ground black pepper,
　to season

FOR THE GREEN SAUCE
3 garlic cloves, peeled
leaves from a small bunch of fresh
　parsley
½ small green fresh chilli/chile
　pepper, seeds removed
1 teaspoon dried oregano
200 ml/scant 1 cup Spanish extra
　virgin olive oil
sea salt and ground black pepper,
　to season

SERVES 2

To prepare the Red Sauce, pound the garlic, cumin seeds, cayenne pepper and pimentón using a mortar and pestle. Start adding the olive oil, little by little, to blend with the rest of the ingredients. Season with salt to taste and set aside.

Prepare the Green Sauce in the same way and set aside.

To prepare the meat, make small incisions vertically all along the pork fillet, leaving 1 cm/½ inch between each incision. You may need to cut the fillet into 2 pieces.

Place the fillet on a hot griddle pan or preheated barbecue grill with the incisions facing down, and cook until it takes on some colour. Turn over, season with salt and cook for about 5 minutes until the pork takes on a golden colour all over. Serve with the sauces and sliced fried potatoes.

Carrilleras de cerdo al vino de Ronda

PORK CHEEKS IN RONDA WINE

Pork cheeks cooked in wine are a true delicacy. The tenderness of good-quality pork meat, when cooked properly, is unequalled. These are normally cooked with sherry but in this recipe, which I developed when teaching at a cookery school near Ronda, I decided to use some of the local wines. They are getting better and better.

1.5 kg/3¼ lb. pork cheeks, cleaned
plain/all-purpose flour, for dusting
3–4 tablespoons Spanish extra
  virgin olive oil
3–4 pieces of lemon peel without
  pith
2 bay leaves
1 cinnamon stick
2 large white onions, chopped
1 large carrot, peeled and chopped
1 x 750-ml bottle Ronda red wine
  (a Rioja Crianza makes a good
  alternative)
sea salt and freshly ground black
  pepper, to season

SERVES 6

Preheat the oven to 160°C/140°C fan/325°F/Gas 3.

Remove any excess fat from the cheeks and cut horizontally in half. Spread some flour on a plate and very lightly coat each cheek, shaking to remove excess. Season with salt and black pepper.

Heat the olive oil in a frying pan/skillet over a medium heat and fry the meat in batches, cooking until golden brown on both sides. Drain each piece on kitchen paper to remove excess oil from the pan, then place in a large flameproof and ovenproof dish with the citrus peel, bay leaves and cinnamon stick. Reserve at a low heat.

In the same frying pan, adding a little more oil if needed, sauté the onions and carrot until softened. Add this to the meat in the ovenproof dish and pour in the wine. Place the ovenproof dish over a medium heat and bring to the boil. Cover and bake in the oven for about 2 hours or until the meat is deliciously tender and the sauce has turned the colour of dark chocolate. Serve with potatoes cooked in your favourite way.

Codornices con uvas

QUAILS WITH GRAPES

It was in a small restaurant outside the enchanting town of Gaucín, in the Sierras of Málaga, where I tasted this lovely dish. At the time, I had been invited by Sally von Meister and Anna Wright to teach Spanish food and wine courses at their cookery school. One evening at the restaurant the cook decided to treat us by including this original recipe in the menu. Unfortunately, the restaurant is long gone now, but I still prepare this dish following the recipe given to me by the cook, a generous woman. I always ensure I follow her instructions to the letter.

8 quails
8 streaky bacon rashers/slices
100 g/3½ oz. spring onions/
   scallions (cebollitas), chopped
150 g/5½ oz. mushrooms, cleaned
   and chopped
2 small carrots, peeled and chopped
1 white onion, chopped
75 g/¾ stick butter
2 tablespoons lard or bacon fat
200 g/7 oz. white seedless grapes,
   peeled
4–5 whole black peppercorns
a pinch of freshly grated nutmeg
250 ml/1 cup dry white wine
120 ml/½ cup Spanish brandy
   'de Jerez'
2 garlic cloves, crushed

SERVES 4–6

Preheat the oven to 180°C/160°C fan/350°F/Gas 4.

Wrap each quail in a rasher/slice of bacon and place them in a large ovenproof dish without overlapping. Add the spring onions/scallions, mushrooms, carrots and onion.

Melt the butter and the lard or bacon fat in a saucepan and pour it over the quails and vegetables in the dish. Cook in the preheated oven for about 15 minutes – by then the bacon will have started sizzling.

Meanwhile, using a large pestle and mortar, pound half the grapes with the peppercorns and the nutmeg and then blend with the wine, brandy and garlic. Remove the quails and vegetables from the oven and pour this mixture over the top. Return the dish to the still-hot oven to cook for a further 45–50 minutes, basting from time to time. Add the remaining grapes. Drain the juices into a saucepan and bring to the boil to reduce a little.

The quails can be served individually or arranged on a serving dish with some of the grapes scattered around them and some sauce drizzled over the top.

Albóndigas preparadas con béchamel en salsa rubia
MEATBALLS MADE WITH BÉCHAMEL IN A BLONDE SAUCE

This recipe has been in my family since the 19th century. It is perfect to cook in the winter in El Zauzal. Béchamel sauce is used in the meatballs in place of the traditional soaked bread as it brings a soft texture, extra flavour and richness.

FOR THE BÉCHAMEL SAUCE
20 g/1½ tablespoons butter
1½ tablespoons plain/all-purpose flour
400 ml/1¾ cups whole/full-fat milk, warm
2–3 grates of fresh nutmeg, to taste
sea salt

FOR THE MEATBALLS
1 white onion, finely chopped
2 garlic cloves, finely chopped
2 tablespoons Spanish olive oil, plus extra for frying
500 g/1 lb. 2 oz. minced/ground pork
500 g/1 lb. 2 oz. minced/ground beef
1½ tablespoons freshly chopped parsley
2 egg yolks
sea salt and freshly ground black pepper, to season
plain/all-purpose flour, for coating
freshly chopped parsley, to garnish

FOR THE BLONDE SAUCE
1½ tablespoons plain/all-purpose flour
2 tablespoons Spanish olive oil
½ a white onion, finely chopped
150 ml/⅔ cup white wine
700 ml/3 cups good-quality beef stock
sea salt, to season

SERVES 6

To prepare the béchamel sauce, melt the butter over a low heat in a small saucepan. Add the flour, little by little, mixing to make a creamy paste. Keep cooking, stirring constantly, for a few minutes. Add the milk, little by little, stirring continually. Season with salt and nutmeg and cook, stirring, for 10–15 minutes, or until the sauce is thick and bubbles with large, volcanic-type bubbles. Cook for another 8 minutes or so, stirring continually. It should be quite thick. Set aside.

For the meatballs, sauté the onions and garlic in a small pan in the olive oil over a low heat, until the onions are tender and translucent.

Put the minced/ground meats in a mixing bowl. Add the parsley, season with salt and pepper and mix well. Add the onion, garlic and egg yolks and mix. Spoon in the béchamel and mix it gently into the meat until the sauce has been completely absorbed. Divide the mixture into 4 parts and then each part into 5–6 portions. Form each portion into small balls.

Place the flour in a bowl and coat the meatballs lightly, one by one, shaking off any excess flour. Over a high heat in a deep frying pan/skillet, heat oil to about one-quarter the height of the meatballs. When hot, gently put as many of the meatballs as you can fit in the pan without them touching each other and fry for 3–4 minutes until light brown, turning only once. Set aside.

To prepare the blonde sauce, toast the flour in a small pan over a low heat until a light golden brown, stirring constantly, so it does not burn. In another pan big enough to hold all the meatballs, heat the olive oil over a medium heat and sauté the onion until light brown. Stir the flour over the onion and cook for a few minutes. Add the wine and the stock (reserving a little stock in case it's needed at the end), little by little, stirring to mix well. Cook for 5–6 minutes more. It should be light at the end.

Add the meatballs and shake the pan gently several times to ensure that they are coated all over. Cover the pan, turn the heat down and cook for 35–40 minutes or until the sauce has a full flavour and is the consistency you like (adding some of the reserved stock if needed).

The meatballs can be served with mashed potatoes, 'fideo' pasta (see page 122) or rice as preferred. Garnish with the parsley before serving.

Rabo de toro, una receta tradicional
OXTAIL, A TRADITIONAL RECIPE

I last tasted this amazing recipe in a restaurant in Málaga city. The meat was as tender as butter, lightly covered with a thin layer of a chocolate-coloured sauce as complex and delicious as ever. The meat that had been removed from the bones was served with the creamiest mashed potatoes you could find. I know why the chef had discarded the bones; the dish looked more appetizing and modern, but for those like me who prefer to enjoy the flavour of the meat attached to the bone, it was a pity. I always favour keeping them in for the most flavour.

1 whole oxtail (weighing about 1–1.2 kg/¼–2¾ lb.), cut into pieces
plain/all-purpose flour, for coating
75 ml/⅓ cup Spanish olive oil
sea salt, to season

FOR THE MARINADE
8 garlic cloves, unpeeled and halved
½ large white onion, chopped
2–3 pieces of lemon or orange peel without pith
1 bay leaf, broken in half
1 teaspoon fresh rosemary leaves
1 teaspoon fresh thyme leaves
4 whole black peppercorns
3 aromatic cloves
750 ml/3¼ cups good-quality Spanish red wine
sea salt, to season

FOR THE SOFRITO
1 white onion, roughly chopped
2 carrots, peeled and cut into rounds
1 large green (bell) pepper, deseeded and chopped
1 large red (bell) pepper, deseeded and chopped
4 garlic cloves, roughly chopped
1 large tomato, chopped
1 bay leaf

SERVES 4

Start preparing this dish the night before you plan to serve it. In a bowl, combine all the marinade ingredients and add the oxtail. Cover and let it marinate overnight in the fridge. Once marinated, remove the meat from the bowl and pat dry with kitchen paper. Season with salt and set aside. Strain and reserve the wine from the marinade and discard the rest.

Coat the meat very lightly in flour. Heat the olive oil in a large saucepan. When hot, start adding the meat to sauté. Turn several times until it is a light gold colour, then remove from the pan. Pat dry with kitchen paper to remove some of the fat. Set aside

Next prepare the sofrito. In the pan used to sauté the meat with some of the oil, add the onion to cook for a few minutes before adding the rest of the ingredients, except the tomato and bay leaf. Cook for about 8 minutes, stirring constantly. Add the tomato. Cook for another 6 minutes and then add 250 ml/1 cup of the reserved wine. Let the alcohol evaporate for a couple of minutes, then add the meat and cover with 1 litre/4 cups water. Add the bay leaf and adjust the seasoning. Bring to the boil, reduce to a moderate heat and simmer, covered, for about 3–4 hours or until the meat becomes very tender.

Remove the oxtail and set aside. Using an electric handheld blender, blend the sauce until as thin as possible. You may need to add a little water to loosen. Pass through a chinois (fine mesh conical sieve/strainer). Return the meat to the sauce, stir and cook uncovered for another 5–8 minutes. Remove from the heat.

One thing I learned from an Andalucian cook is once ready, cover the pan and allow the oxtail to rest overnight or for at least for 10 hours. Reheat before serving. Mashed potatoes are ideal to accompany this rich and flavoursome stew.

Potage de lentejas con chorizo y panceta
LENTIL STEW WITH CHORIZO & CURED BELLY OF PORK

Lentils are one of the pulses/legumes on which my generation was raised, served both at home and at school. Today, it's my son Daniel who has inherited a taste for lentils, and he often cooks them at our home in Aracena following a local recipe. He buys his lentils at the same time as he buys cooking chorizo and a deliciously cured 'panceta de Ibérico'. I like to use the Spanish Pardina variety for this recipe, which are a greenish-brown colour and slightly smaller than French Puy lentils.

Arreglo is the word used for a mixture added at the end of the recipe to enhance the flavour of the ingredients. Pimentón de La Vera (La Vera is a locality in Extremadura) used in it can be considered a unique ingredient that defines a multitude of dishes cooked all over Spain as well as a fundamental ingredient in the making of chorizo and other cured meats.

300 g/1¾ cups dried green lentils (such as *Pardina*)
½ white onion, peeled
2 garlic cloves, unpeeled
1 carrot, peeled and cut into rounds
½ green (bell) pepper, halved and deseeded
100 g/3½ oz. chorizo sausage in one piece
100 g/3½ oz. smoked or cured panceta
a splash of Spanish olive oil
1 bay leaf
4–5 whole black peppercorns
sea salt, to season

FOR THE ARREGLO
2 tablespoons Spanish olive oil
2 garlic cloves, halved
1 teaspoon *Pimentón de la Vera* (Spanish hot smoked paprika)

SERVES 4

Put the lentils in a bowl and cover with cold water. Soak overnight or for at least 4 hours.

Drain and rinse the soaked lentils in fresh running water. Place them in a large saucepan just covered with cold water. Add the onion, garlic, carrot, green (bell) pepper, chorizo, panceta, a splash of olive oil, the bay leaf and the peppercorns.

Bring to the boil, cover and simmer gently for about 30–40 minutes or until both the lentils and the meats are tender. As the lentils swell when cooking, you may need to add some more cold water if the liquid has reduced too much. Check often as they can catch and burn very easily. When ready set aside.

Meanwhile prepare the arreglo. Heat the oil in small frying pan/skillet. When hot, add the garlic and cook until it begins to take colour. Remove the pan from the heat and quickly add the paprika. Stir and let it rest for 30 seconds to infuse and give a lovely colour to the oil. Pour the oil and the garlic over the lentils, leaving behind the sediment of the paprika.

Remove the bay leaf and the peppercorns from the lentils if you can find them! Cut the chorizo and the panceta into pieces. Return them to the pan with the lentils and heat through before serving. Don't allow them to dry out.

FOR THOSE WITH A SWEET TOOTH

A World of Sweet Things

Honey, then sugar, brought from Africa by Islamic merchants to the Iberian Peninsula in the Middle Ages, forever changed the world of sweet things in Spain, especially as sugar cane was then planted in the province of Alicante in the east of the country and in subtropical Andalucía, in the province of Granada. Soon it would cross the Atlantic, becoming a part of the Colombian Exchange. By the 16th century, sugar produced in the Americas would be unloaded at the port of Sevilla.

I love to use the term 'recipes from the past' as they refer to the rich legacy left, particularly but not exclusively, by medieval Islamic and Jewish cooks in Andalucía, preserved in two manuscripts dating back to the 12th and 13th centuries. These recipes have also been handed down by word of mouth in monasteries and convents, from cook to cook, and from century to century. In addition to this, convent kitchens were also the recipients of sweet recipes brought by noble widows retiring to a monastic life but still wishing to be fed there by their own cooks with the recipes they were familiar with. The aromatic *Alfajor* now so popular in Argentina and of Spanish origin, is one of the many Spanish recipes with an extraordinary past (see page 168).

To fully understand the complexity of *La Cocina Dulce Andaluza* (the sweet cooking of Andalucía) we have to distinguish between the professional cook, the monastic cook and the home cook. A *pastelero* or *pastelería* is a professional pastry chef working in

a *pastelería* (cake shop), in an hotel or a restaurant and using traditional or modern recipes. The monastic cook can also be considered as a professional, as the cooking is at a professional level even if they never professionally trained. Monastic cooks are also the guardians of many recipes from the past. Home cooks feed their families with local recipes, recipes inherited from their mothers and grandmothers or today, increasingly from what they see on the television or come across online.

Andalucians have a very sweet tooth, which is why it is perhaps not surprising to come across so very many *pastelerías* in every city and town. Not far from El Paseo, the main square in Aracena where we have our home, is *Casa Rufino*. It is one of the most prestigious and beautifully decorated shops in the Sierra, specializing in fine quality *pastelería* and traditional recipes as well as wedding cakes. Here the *Almendrados* (see page 160), *Torrijas* (see page 164), and *Brazo 'de Gitano'* (see page 171) are all truly delicious. Nearby, excellent artisanal breads and other breads made with sweet enriched doughs are baked in *El Molinillo*. This is where I like to buy *Magdalenas Caseras*, which my family all adore. Spanish *magdalenas* differ from French madeleine cakes in that they are prepared with olive oil instead

of butter. I have one last recommendation to share – when in Sevilla I urge you to try some Yemas, a unique egg confection prepared by nuns in the kitchens of the 14th Century Covent of *San Clemente*.

I have tried to include sweet recipes belonging to both the past and the present in this chapter of the book. Some, learned from people in different parts of the region, some from convent cooks, others from avantgarde chefs but also from my own Andalucian adventures in the kitchen. I have also learned how strongly related these recipes are with the rich Catholic calendar of saints days and festivals, such as Christmas and Holy Week, when special recipes are made at home and offered in *panaderías* (bakeries) and *pastelerías* around the region.

Almendrados
ALMOND & APRICOT COOKIES

I have to dedicate this recipe to my dearest friend Carolina Mier, who spoke Spanish with the loveliest Andalucian accent. In September every year she brought not only delicious jams to our home El Zauzal, but also several kilograms of the sweetest almonds from her own garden. She particularly loved this recipe.

250 g/2½ cups ground almonds
250 g/1¾ cups icing/confectioners' sugar, plus extra for dusting
finely grated zest of ½ a lemon
1 teaspoon runny honey
3 medium/US large egg whites, beaten to soft peaks
60 g/scant ½ cup chopped dried apricots (optional)

a baking sheet lined with baking paper

MAKES 18

In a bowl, mix the almonds and icing/confectioners' sugar. Add the lemon zest, honey and beaten egg whites in three batches, blend well each time to obtain an almond dough. Leave it to rest, covered, for 1½ hours.

Divide the dough into 18 pieces and shape them with your hands into rounds. Coat each one with icing sugar and press a piece of chopped apricot on top, if using. Place them on a baking sheet lined with baking paper and leave them to rest for another 2 hours.

Preheat the oven to 200°C/180°C fan/400°F/Gas 6 and bake for about 8 minutes or until they take some colour. Be careful as they can burn easily. Dust with a little icing sugar before serving.

Helado de vainilla y turrón con pasas en vino moscatel

SOFT NOUGAT ICE CREAM WITH RAISINS IN MOSCATEL

If you like sweet desserts this is one full of Eastern pleasures made with a list of ingredients that would be hard to match: Málaga raisins known as *pasas*, sweet Málaga wine and a delicious ice cream made with vanilla and a soft nutty *turrón*, also homemade. In Spain, soft turrón, known by the generic name of '*Jijona*', is associated with Christmas, although it can be found in markets all year around. It is made with almonds, honey, sugar and lemon zest. Jijona is a town in Alicante where this type of turrón originates. You will need to soak the raisins or *Pasas de Málaga* in sweet Málaga wine for at least two days before using them in this recipe.

FOR THE RAISINS IN MOSCATEL
6 tablespoons raisins or
  Pasas de Malaga
375 ml/½ a 75-cl bottle sweet
  Malaga wine (I use *Jorge Ordoñez
  Seleccion Especial*)

FOR THE SOFT TURRÓN
300 g/2⅓ cups peeled and
  toasted almonds
250 g/1 cup runny honey
100 g/½ cup granulated/white
  sugar
1 teaspoon finely grated lemon zest

FOR THE ICE CREAM BASE
1 vanilla pod/bean
500 ml/2 cups whole/full-fat milk
6 egg yolks
250 ml/1 cup whipping cream
  or double/heavy cream
150 g/5½ oz. Soft Turrón
  (see above) or ready-made
  Jijona turron

a 15 x 22-cm/6 x 8½-inch baking
  pan, lined with baking paper
an ice cream maker

SERVES 6

First prepare the raisins. Soak them in the sweet wine for at least 2 days before you plan to make the ice cream.

To prepare the soft turrón, coarsely grind the prepared almonds using an electric blender.

In a large saucepan, heat the honey over a very low heat. With a wooden spoon, stir gently for at least 40 minutes for the water content to evaporate. Add the sugar and carry on stirring until it becomes a soft dough. Add the almonds and stir energetically until fully integrated into the dough. Pour the turrón into the prepared pan and cover with another piece of baking paper. Top with a baking weight or something heavy to press down on the turron so that it releases some of the almond oil. Leave it to rest for about 2 hours.

To make the ice cream base, split the vanilla pod in half lengthways and scrape out the seeds with the tip of a sharp knife. Put the pods in a large saucepan. Pour the milk into the saucepan and bring just to boiling point. Put the egg yolks into a bowl and beat. Pour the hot milk over the eggs, stir until smooth, then pour back into the pan. Reduce the heat and cook over low heat, stirring contstantly with a wooden spoon, until the custard has thickened. Cover and chill for 15 minutes. Using an electric hand whisk, whip the cream until forming soft peaks and then stir it into the cooled custard. Use a spatula to fold in the soft and oily turrón.

Let the ice cream mixture cool completely, then churn in an ice cream maker, following the manufacturer's instructions.

Pour the soaked raisins and juices over portions of the ice cream to serve.

Torrijas de siempre
CLASSIC SPANISH-STYLE 'FRENCH TOAST'

Torrijas, a classic recipe associated with Easter, have always been prepared by home cooks or sold in *pastelerías*, bars and restaurants. Depending on the region, you will find them made with wine or milk. Once fried, they are coated with sugar syrup and then with cinnamon sugar. Having become very popular, modern chefs are now offering *torrijas* on their menus prepared with different types of bread, which they cut into various shapes. In addition they also serve them with a multitude of delicious toppings. This is the original classic recipe using milk.

1.5 litres/1½ quarts whole/full-fat milk
peel from ½ a lemon
½ vanilla pod/bean, split lengthwise
1 small cinnamon stick
1 old-fashioned baguette from the previous day, cut into thick slices
4 large/US extra-large eggs
150 g/¾ cup white/granulated sugar, plus extra for coating
1 teaspoon ground cinnamon
Spanish olive oil for frying, nothing too strong flavoured
vanilla or coconut ice cream, to serve (optional)

MAKES 8-10 SLICES

Heat the milk (do not let it boil) in a saucepan. Add the sugar and stir. When dissolved, remove the milk from the heat and add the lemon peel, vanilla pod/bean and the cinnamon stick. Leave the milk to infuse for 10 minutes, after which time remove the lemon, vanilla and cinnamon. Set the milk aside.

Start arranging slices of bread in a single layer in a large rectangular ovenproof dish. Pour over the infused milk so that the bread is well covered. Add another layer of bread on top and cover with the rest of the milk, making certain it is all well soaked. Leave to rest for 30 minutes.

Place the sugar and ground cinnamon in a flat dish, mix well and set aside. Crack the eggs into a shallow bowl and beat.

Heat the olive oil in a large frying pan/skillet until hot, but not smoking, start adding the milky 'torrijas'. Lift a slice of the soaked bread out of the dish, and coat it in the beaten eggs, before placing in the hot pan. Do not overlap them in the pan. You will need to turn them once or twice as they start taking colour. Remove and place them on kitchen paper while you cook the rest.

Traditionally torrijas are served dipped first in a sugar syrup and then coated with cinnamon sugar. I prefer to eat them without the syrup, just lightly sprinkled with the cinnamon and sugar and served with a scoop of vanilla or coconut ice cream on the side.

Flan de naranja sanguina y caramelo
BLOOD ORANGE & CARAMEL BAKED CUSTARDS

I love a good Spanish flan. Apart from a yummy rice pudding, my father's irresistible *Flan de Caramelo* (crème caramel) was the only thing he would cook with certain regularity (in the kitchen, he could not compete with my mother). He had a very sweet tooth and he was partial to the *Flan de Naranja*. Sometimes he added a little milk but if the orange juice was particularly delicious he would omit it. When in season, the blood orange is utterly delicious, although a good orange flan can be made with any fresh orange juice that has a touch of lively acidity.

600 ml/2½ cups freshly squeezed blood orange juice
200 g/1 cup caster/superfine sugar
grated zest from ½ an orange
8 large/US extra-large egg yolks
2 medium/US large eggs

FOR THE CARAMEL
150 g/¾ cup caster/superfine sugar

6 crème caramel moulds or other suitably sized ramekin dishes
an ovenproof baking dish, large enough to take the 6 moulds

MAKES 6

Preheat the oven to 180°C/160°C fan/350°F/Gas 4.

First make the caramel. Place the sugar and 150 ml/⅔ cup water in a saucepan. Start heating over a medium heat to dissolve the sugar completely. Increase the heat and bring to the boil without stirring. Cook rapidly until the syrup has taken a brick colour. Remove from the heat and pour carefully over the bottom and the sides of each mould. Place the moulds in a baking dish and set aside.

Place the orange juice, sugar and orange zest in another saucepan. Stir to dissolve the sugar in the water. Slowly bring to the boil, then reduce the heat to a very gentle simmer. Cook for a few minutes more, then remove from the heat and set aside.

Use a metal whisk to blend the egg yolks and whole eggs in a large bowl. Sieve/strain the sugary orange juice then add to the eggs. Stir and sieve into a jug/pitcher and pour into each mould. Pour boiling water into the baking dish, to come halfway up the sides of each mould. Cover the dish with aluminium foil and cook in the preheated oven for about 1 hour until the flans are set.

Remove the moulds from the water, leave to cool down, then place in the fridge for a couple of hours or even better overnight before serving.

Alfajores Andaluces de Navidad

CHRISTMAS SPICE COOKIES

Not so long ago, a whole repertoire of traditional sweet things were prepared by home cooks all over Andalucía to celebrate Christmas. Following ancient recipes with promising nutty and spice aromas from the Middle East, many of these recipes have been kept alive today in the kitchens of monasteries and convents, as well as in local *pastelerías* (cake shops) where customers are prepared to queue for a long time before they all sell out. To illustrate the above, I have selected a recipe for *alfajores*, which I believe is very representative of the rich cultural legacy left behind in Al-Andalus by talented Islamic cooks.

320 g/generous 1½ cups caster/superfine sugar

200 g/1½ cups whole hazelnuts, peeled

250 g/scant 2 cups whole almonds, peeled

50 g/⅓ cup sesame seeds

1 aromatic clove, pounded

1 g teaspoon coriander seeds (about 50 seeds)

400 g/1½ cups runny honey

250 g/3 cups fine dry breadcrumbs

a small piece of orange peel pith removed

icing/confectioners' sugar mixed with ground cinnamon, to dust

MAKES ABOUT 35

Place 120 g/generous ½ cup of the caster/superfine sugar and 120 ml/½ cup water in a small saucepan over a medium heat. Swirl the pan to dissolve the sugar. Bring to the boil to form a light syrup. Remove from the heat and set aside.

Toast the nuts in a frying pan/skillet. Set aside and, in the same pan, toast the sesame seeds and the coriander seeds, very carefully, just for a few seconds, then set aside.

Blend the nuts in a food processor. Remove and set aside, and then add the spices to the food processor and blend those.

Place the honey in a medium saucepan, bring to the boil, then remove from the heat. Add the spices, stir them in using a small spatula. Add the nuts, mix again, before adding the breadcrumbs. Mix once more and start very slowly pouring in the sugar syrup, working constantly to obtain a pliable dough.

Place this dough on a flat surface and while the dough is still warm, divide into 40 g/1½ oz. portions. Shape into small, equal-sized cylinders, pressing the top and bottom with your index finger and thumb.

Prepare another sugar syrup as above in a small saucepan, by heating 200 ml/scant 1 cup water with the remaining sugar and the orange peel to infuse it with flavour. Let the syrup cool down, then remove the peel.

Coat each alfajore with the orange-infused sugar syrup and let them drip on a wire cooling rack with a sheet of baking paper underneath before coating them in cinnamon icing/confectioners' sugar. Let them dry completely for about 24 hours, then wrap them in white tissue paper or baking paper and store in an airtight container. They will keep for a week or so.

Brazo 'de gitano'
ORANGE CREAM-FILLED ROULADE

This intriguing name, 'gypsy's arm' in Spanish refers to a roulade (rolled sponge cake) that can be prepared with different types of sweet or savoury fillings. For this recipe I have used oranges picked from our own trees in El Zauzal. It has become another treat to remember when baking in the darker days of winter.

FOR THE ROULADE SPONGE

3 large/US extra-large eggs, separated
80 g/⅓ cup white caster/superfine sugar
80 g/⅔ cup plain/all-purpose flour
seeds from ½ vanilla pod/bean split lengthwise
freshly squeezed juice of ½ an orange
finely grated zest of ½ orange

FOR THE FILLING

175 g/6 oz. full-fat cream cheese
80 g/⅓ cup condensed milk
100 g/scant ½ cup double/heavy cream
freshly squeezed juice of ½ an orange

TO FINISH

finely grated zest of ½ an orange
icing/confectioners' sugar, for dusting

30 x 45-cm/12 x 20-inch baking pan greased and lined with baking paper
a second piece of baking paper, the same size as the baking pan

SERVES 6

Preheat the oven to 190°C/170°C fan/375°F/Gas 5.

Place the egg whites in a bowl and use an electric hand whisk to start working the egg whites to peaks.

Halfway through start adding the sugar, little by little, and continue to mix to a meringue consistency.

Use a spatula to carefully fold in the egg yolks, one by one, followed by the rest of the roulade ingredients. Pour into the prepared baking pan and use the spatula to level the surface.

Bake in the preheated oven for about 15 minutes, making certain the batter has been cooked completely. Leave it to cool down before removing from the pan.

While the batter is baking, start preparing the filling. Whisk the cream cheese, condensed milk, cream and orange juice to a creamy texture.

Place the second piece of baking paper on top of the cooled roulade base. Carefully turn over and gently peel off the bottom layer of baking paper (which is now on top).

Pour the cream cheese mixture over the base and use a spatula to spread over the whole surface. Use the baking paper underneath to start rolling the base as tightly as possible, until it becomes a perfect roll. By then the paper will be in your hands.

Place the roulade in a rectangular serving dish and sprinkle with icing/confectioners' sugar and orange zest to finish. Serve as soon as possible (the roulade should not be placed in the fridge to chill). It is delicious served with a scoop of vanilla ice cream or with a little fresh single/light cream for pouring.

Arroz con leche cremoso
CREAMY RICE PUDDING

In Andalucía, many restaurants include *arroz con leche* (rice pudding) on the menus and these days, a creamier version called *arroz con leche cremoso* is often a speciality of the house. This variation takes longer to prepare but is worth every single extra minute spent stirring the rice. It is so moreish.

150 g/1 cup Spanish round rice
  (I love Bomba for this recipe)
1.5 litres/6 cups whole/full-fat milk
1 cinnamon stick
peel of 1 small lemon, washed, pith
  removed
35g/2 tablespoons butter
150 g/¾ cup caster/granulated sugar,
  plus extra if needed
ground cinnamon, to sprinkle (optional)
6 small dessert dishes, enamel 'paella'
  pans or traditional cazuelitas

SERVES 6

Bring 1 litre/4 cups water to the boil in a saucepan. Add the rice and boil for 4–5 minutes. Drain through a sieve/strainer, discard the water and reserve the rice.

In the same pan, heat the milk over a low heat. Add the cinnamon stick and the lemon peel and leave to infuse for several minutes, then remove the peel and the cinnamon. Return to the heat, bring to the boil and add the part-boiled rice. Reduce the heat and stir occasionally for about 1 hour.

Add the butter and stir well before adding the sugar, a little at a time, until it dissolves completely. Stir constantly as it catches easily. By now the rice should be very soft, tasty and creamy. Pour into serving dishes of choice. Best served cold from the fridge.

NOTE *This can be finished sprinkled with ground cinnamon or with sugar caramelized with a chefs' blowtorch or under a preheated grill/broiler.*

Manzanas al jugo de manzana, especias y almendras tostadas
APPLES IN APPLE JUICE, SPICES & TOASTED ALMONDS

Spice and herb sellers can be found in many Andalucian local markets, always prepared to give advice on this complex subject and share recipes. In Barbate, a fisherman's port close to Cádiz, I bought the freshest cinnamon sticks, white cardamom and saffron to prepare a very easy recipe celebrating the arrival of spring in Aracena. I recommend sourcing a good-quality unsweetened apple juice for this dish.

4 sweet apples, peeled
1 litre/4 cups unsweetened apple juice
sugar, to taste
1 small cinnamon stick
2 green cardamom pods
a few saffron filaments, pounded and
  dissolved in a little hot water
a small handful of toasted flaked/
  slivered almonds
4 fresh mint leaves (optional),
  to garnish
crème fraîche or sour cream, to serve

SERVES 4

Place the apples in a saucepan with the apple juice and some sugar to taste. Gently heat until the sugar has dissolved, then add the spices. Bring to the boil. Cook the apples for about 30 minutes, or until they become just tender.

Use a slotted spoon to remove the apples from the liquid. Reserve the liquid, discarding the spices. Return the juice to the heat, bring to the boil and reduce until a light apple syrup. Leave to cool.

Serve the apples in some of the apple syrup topped with a sprinkle of flaked almonds and a small mint leaf, if liked, and a bowl of crème fraîche on the side.

Flan de calabaza y caramelo
BUTTERNUT SQUASH CARAMEL FLAN

María José Moreno who lives across the road from us in Aracena, is a generous and brilliant cook with whom to share recipes, delicious lunches and dinners. I tasted this recipe for the first time in María José's kitchen and I thought it was so pleasant with such a unique texture so I am sharing it with you here. *(Pictured on page 175.)*

1.3 kg/3 lb. butternut squash
200 g/1 scant cup sunflower oil
500 g/2½ cups caster/superfine sugar
3 g/½ teaspoon cornflour/cornstarch
1 teaspoon baking power
4 medium/US large eggs
60 g/½ cup plain/all-purpose flour, sifted

FOR THE LIQUID CARAMEL
400 g/2 cups caster/superfine sugar
200 ml/1 cup cold water
200 ml/1 scant cup hot water blended with a few drops of lemon juice

a kitchen thermometer
a 30 x 20 x 4-cm/12 x 8 x 2-inch baking pan, greased

SERVES 8

First, prepare the liquid caramel. Pour the sugar and cold water into a medium wide-based pan. Place over a low heat to dissolve the sugar. Increase the heat and bring to the boil. Boil until the temperature reaches 194°C/381°F. Do not stir. Very carefully, as it could spit, pour half the hot water and lemon juice on the caramel. It will start boiling even faster. Add the remaining hot water and lemon juice. Stir with a metal whisk for a couple of minutes and the liquid caramel will be ready. Leave to cool down properly.

Preheat the oven to 220°C/200°C fan/425°F/Gas 7.

Peel and cut the squash into pieces and place in a saucepan. Cover with boiling water and cook until tender. Drain well, making sure the squash pulp is fairly dry. Set aside.

Place the squash and all the remaining ingredients, except the caramel, in a food processor and blend to a creamy texture. Transfer to the prepared baking pan and bake in the preheated oven for 35–40 minutes. Remove from the oven and leave to cool completely.

Pour the cooled liquid caramel over the top and chill until ready to serve. Cut into squares and serve on its own, with a scoop of vanilla ice cream or fresh cream for pouring, as preferred.

NOTE *This liquid caramel (caramelo líquido) can be stored in an airtight container in the fridge for up to 1 month.*

Limonada y granizado de limón
ZESTY LEMONADE & LEMON GRANITA

Who can resist a full glass of lemonade in the middle of the summer and what about a full glass of lemon granita after dinner? Unlike orange trees, lemon trees yield lemons all year round and in Andalucía there are lemon trees everywhere. You can buy lemons just as they come from the trees, very juicy and unwaxed. *Granizados are the old sorbets of Al-Andalus, which were made with spicy honey, flavoured with cloves and cinnamon.* (*Pictured on pages 178–179.*)

3 large unwaxed lemons, washed
300 g/1½ cups caster/superfine
  sugar
fresh mint leaves, to garnish
  (optional)

MAKES 1.5 LITRES/1½ QUARTS

TO MAKE LEMONADE
Grate the zest of one of the lemons into a bowl. Cut all the lemons in half and squeeze the juice into the bowl. Add the squeezed lemon halves to the bowl with the zest and juice. Add 1.5 litres/1½ quarts water, stir and press the lemons as much as possible. Leave to macerate for 35 minutes. Sieve/strain into a glass jar. Add two-thirds of the sugar and then more to taste if needed. Stir well, then place in the fridge until ready to serve.

TO MAKE LEMON GRANITA
Follow the same method as for Lemonade (see above) but instead of pouring the lemonade into a glass jar, pour into a light, freezerproof rectangular dish and place in the freezer for 30 minutes.

Remove from the freezer. By now some of the top should have converted into ice. Use the tines of a fork to break the ice by punching the surface and blending at the same time with the rest of the liquid. Return to the freezer for another 30 minutes and do the same again. Return it again to the freezer and repeat the freezing and blending until you have a truly fluffy granita.

Serve in pretty glasses such as the old traditional-style Champagne coupes. Add a little mint leaf to each glass before serving.

Tarta de queso y pistachio en masa filo 'el Albaicín'

FILO CHEESECAKE WITH PISTACHIOS FROM ALBAICÍN

**There are very few dishes in Spain that can be considered a National Dish –
La Tortilla de Patata, El Gazpacho Andaluz, El Cocido and *La Paella* – and yet, in
the last few years, a cheesecake originating in the Basque Country, *El Pastel Vasco*,
is on the way to becoming another one. This recipe is a variation made with filo/
phyllo pastry and fresh pistachios, ingredients that hail from the Middle East.**

270 g/9½ oz. readymade filo/
   phyllo pastry
150 g/⅔ stick unsalted butter,
   very soft
300 g/1¼ cups fresh double/
   heavy cream
400 g/14 oz. full-fat cream cheese
50 g/scant ¼ cup sour cream or
   natural/plain yogurt
1 teaspoon vanilla bean paste
finely grated orange zest, to taste
freshly squeezed juice of ½ a lemon
freshly squeezed juice of ½ a small
   orange
3 medium/US large eggs
75 g/⅓ cup caster/superfine sugar
50 g/⅓ cup peeled pistachio
   kernels, ground (reserve
   a few to garnish) (see Note)
dried rose petals, to garnish
   (optional)

*a 24-cm/9½-inch round baking
   pan with removable base*

SERVES 8–10

Preheat the oven to 170°C/150°C fan/325°F/Gas 3.

Unpack the filo/phyllo pastry. Take one of the sheets and cover the rest
with a cloth to stop the pastry drying. This is important. Place on the work
surface. Using a pastry brush, brush the filo pastry surface with the butter,
turn over and brush the other side. Filo pastry is very fragile and may
crack or break but don't worry, use the pieces all the same. Place the first
layer in the prepared baking pan, leaving 4–5 cm/1½–2 inches resting over
the edge, and press it into the bottom of the pan, so the pastry sits well,
leaving plenty of space at the centre. Work gently but quickly. Do the same
with the rest of the sheets, alternating 90 degrees each time. Bake in the
preheated oven for about 8 minutes until the pastry takes a lovely colour.
Remove from the oven and leave to cool. Reduce the oven temperature
to 160°C/140°C fan/325°F/Gas 3.

Using an electric whisk, whisk the double/heavy cream, sour cream or
yogurt, vanilla, citrus zest and juices, eggs and sugar to a very creamy
texture. Add the ground pistachios and carry on whisking until well mixed.
Pour this mixture over the filo pastry and cover lightly with aluminium foil
to avoid the pastry burning. Bake in the still hot oven for 2 hours. Remove
from the oven and when cool, remove from the pan. Sprinkle with a few
reserved pistachios to finish.

NOTE *You can buy ready peeled pistachios or you will need to remove
their skins at least several hours in advance. To do this, put plenty of water
and ice in a bowl. Bring a saucepan of water to the boil and blanch the
pistachios for a couple of minutes, then drain. Place them in the ice bath
and, when completely cold, the skins should start lifting off. Sieve/strain.
Rub the pistachios in a clean kitchen towel to remove any remaining skins
and dry them. To ensure they are completely dry place them on kitchen
paper and let them air dry for several hours before using them.*

Piononos de Santa Fe

TRADITIONAL CAKES FROM SANTA FE

In Granada I found in every *pastelería* (cake shop) these small intriguing cakes that were completely new to me. The recipe dates back to the 20th century when it was created by a local pastry chef, Ceferino Isla González. I decided to add some lemon, orange juice and a touch of rum, which I think go well.

FOR THE PASTRY CREAM
6 eggs, separated (weigh the eggs without the shells to determine the amount of sugar)
caster/superfine sugar (double the weight of the eggs, see above)
25 g/1 oz. cornflour/cornstarch, sifted
75 ml/⅓ cup whole/full-fat milk
50 ml/scant ¼ cup mixed freshly squeezed lemon and orange juices

FOR THE SPONGE
4 medium/US large eggs, separated
80 g/⅓ cup caster/superfine sugar
30 ml/2 tablespoons whole/full-fat milk
50 g/⅓ cup plain/all-purpose flour
50 g/½ cup cornflour/cornstarch
ground cinnamon, to taste

FOR THE SUGAR SYRUP
150 g/¾ cup caster/superfine sugar
freshly squeezed juice of ½ a lemon
a few tablespoons of rum

30 x 45 cm/12 x 20 inch baking pan, greased and lined with baking paper
a piping/pastry bag

MAKES 6

For the pastry cream, use an electric whisk to beat the egg yolks and sugar in a saucepan until fluffy and white. Add the cornflour/cornstarch and continue beating. Add the milk, a little at a time, then add the lemon and orange juices and blend. Heat over a medium heat, stirring, until the mixture starts to thicken. Remove from the heat and carry on beating until it thickens. Transfer to a shallow dish, cover with clingfilm/plastic wrap, making certain there is no air trapped between the cream and the film. Transfer to the fridge to cool.

Preheat the oven to 220°C/200°C fan/425°F/Gas 7.

Prepare the sponge. Use an electric whisk to beat the egg yolks with half the sugar until they have gained in volume and become whiter in colour. Start adding the milk and carry on beating until fully mixed, then set aside.

In a different bowl, using the electric whisk, beat the egg whites and the rest of the sugar to make a thick meringue. Use a spatula to fold the meringue, a spatula at a time, into the creamy mixture. Add the flour and cornflour a little at a time, to retain as much air as possible.

Fill the prepared baking pan with the batter – 1–2 cm/½–1 inch deep. Spread the batter evenly to the edges with a palette knife. Bake in the preheated oven for 6–7 minutes until it takes a little colour. Leave to cool.

Turn the sponge out, leaving it face down. Carefully remove the baking paper and turn the sponge back over, so it is face up. Trim to a rectangular shape, then cut the sponge into 2 equal pieces.

Make the sugar syrup by heating the sugar and lemon juice with 150 ml/⅔ cup water in a saucepan until it starts boiling. Set aside to cool.

Use a pastry brush to brush the sponge with the syrup and then with the rum. Use a palette knife to cover the whole sponge with a thin layer of the pastry cream. With the help of the paper, start rolling the first piece of sponge into a tight roll. Cut into 4 equal portions. Do the same with the second piece and cut into another 4.

Fill a piping/pastry bag with the remaining pastry cream and cover the top of each pionono with a swirl of it. Sprinkle sugar on each cake and use a chefs' blow torch or hot grill/broiler to caramelize the top.

Hornazo dulce de Huelva

SWEET PIE FROM HUELVA

Hornazos are pies baked in many parts of Spain. Some are savoury and others sweet, following very different recipes in each region. In Huelva, they are traditionally eaten during the two main religious events of the year, Christmas and Easter. They are filled with almonds and a rich filling made from a squash known as *Cabello de Ángel* (angels' hair). See page 189 for the recipe for my Homemade 'Cabello de Ángel' Pumpkin Preserve that is necessary to create this delicious pie, or it can also be purchased in cans already prepared if you prefer.

FOR THE BASE DOUGH

50 ml/3½ tablespoons *Anís del Mono Dulce* (Spanish sweet aniseed liqueur)

1 teaspoon aniseeds

100 ml/scant ½ cup Spanish olive oil

100 ml/scant ½ cup white wine

250 g/1¾ cups plain/all-purpose flour, sifted

7 g/¼ oz. dried yeast

a pinch of fine sea salt

FOR THE FILLING

3 medium/US large eggs

150 g/¾ cup caster/superfine sugar

finely grated zest of 2 lemons

350 g/12½ oz. Homemade 'Cabello de Ángel' Pumpkin Preserve (see page 189) or use a canned product

100 g/1 cup ground almonds

TO DECORATE

100 g/1¼ cups flaked/slivered almonds

1 tablespoon white sesame seeds

ground cinnamon, for sprinkling

icing/confectioners' sugar, for dusting

a baking sheet lined with baking paper

SERVES 10

In a small saucepan, bring the aniseed liqueur, aniseeds, olive oil and wine to the boil, then simmer for a couple of minutes. Remove from the heat, sieve/strain and leave to cool down.

Place the the flour, yeast and salt in a mixing bowl. Start adding, the cooled liquid, little by little, and blend using a metal whisk. Using one hand, gather all the ingredients together and transfer to a flat surface. With your hands start kneading to a very soft, easy to work dough. Set aside.

Use a different bowl to make the filling. Use an electric whisk to beat the eggs with the sugar until fluffy and light in colour. Add the lemon zest and the cinnamon and using a spatula blend gently. Add the Cabello de Angel Preserve and ground almonds and blend again. Set aside.

Preheat the oven to 200°C/180°C fan/400°F/Gas 6.

Place the dough on top of the prepared baking sheet. With the tips of your fingers, extend the dough thinly into a round. Roll up around the edge by just one turn. Add the filling evenly so it sits within the rolled edge and bake in the preheated oven for 45–50 minutes. Leave to cool down completely.

To decorate, toast the almonds in a small frying pan/skillet, stirring constantly. When the almonds start taking colour, add the sesame seeds, just for a few seconds. Leave to cool down.

Decorate the pie with the cooled toasted almonds and sesame seeds, sprinkle over some ground cinnamon and dust with a little icing/confectioners' sugar to finish. Cut into slices to serve.

Pasta de membrillo

QUINCE PASTE

Until twenty or so years ago, very traditional Spanish recipes prepared everywhere, including Andalucía, were almost unknown outside Spain. Today these recipes are present not only in specialist shops but also in main retailers in many parts of the world. *Pan con Membrillo* was a frequent part of our '*la merienda*' (after-school treat), which my mother would give me when I arrived home from school.

Now I love to serve membrillo with fresh or cured goat or sheep's milk cheese, as well as a few walnuts. *(Pictured on page 187.)*

1 kg/2¼ lb. fresh quince, unpeeled
caster/superfine sugar (see method
    for amount needed)

a 20 x 15-cm/8 x 6-inch shallow
    dish, lined with baking paper

MAKES ABOUT 800 G/1¾ LB.

Boil the quinces, unpeeled, in a large saucepan of water for about 50 minutes until very tender. Set aside and let them cool down. Once cool, peel and core the quinces and cut into pieces.

Weigh the chopped quince, and then weigh out the same amount of sugar. Put both in a saucepan and heat until the sugar has been completely dissolved. Remove from the heat.

Use an electric whisk to blend the quince to a very creamy pulp. Return to the heat and cook, stirring almost continuously, for about 50–60 minutes until very thick and glossy. Be very careful while stirring as it may splash.

When ready let the paste cool down for a few minutes. Pour into the prepared dish and leave to set. It will take a couple of hours to solidify completely. Slice into 4 rectangular portions of equal size with a sharp knife. One portion is sufficient to serve 4–6 people as an accompaniment to cheese.

NOTE *To prepare 'membrillo' of a lighter colour, peel and core the quinces before boiling. Whisk and weigh the pulp before adding the sugar. Then proceed as above.*

Cabello de Ángel casero
HOMEMADE 'ANGEL HAIR' PUMPKIN PRESERVE

As a child I did not enjoy *Cabello de Ángel* and I don't know why. Now I think it is delicious, unique and a way to cook pumpkin and make something special. *Cabello de Ángel* is made with the pulp of the cidra squash. It has been successfully added as a filling to a number of pastries and other baked Spanish traditional treats for a long time. In Andalucía, look for *Cortadillos de Cidra* or the Sweet Easter Pie from Huelva, among others. If you do not have access to the cidra squash, they are difficult to find outside Spain, the spaghetti squash is a perfect alternative. Normally, *Cabello de Ángel* is incredibly sweet, so I have decided to reduce the sugar by half in this recipe. Use this in the recipe for Sweet Pie from Huelva on page 185. *(Pictured on page 187.)*

1 cidra or spaghetti squash
caster/superfine sugar
   (see method for weight)
lemon peel, pith removed and
   freshly squeezed juice of
   ½ a lemon

*a 500-ml/18-oz. capacity jar,
sterilized (see page 192)*

MAKES ABOUT 500 G/1 LB. 2 OZ.

To prepare the pulp, carefully cut the squash into large pieces and remove the seeds. Place in a large saucepan and cover with water. Bring to the boil and simmer for about 30 minutes until tender. Drain, reserving the cooking water, then leave the cooked squash to cool down.

Use a fork to remove the pulp from the skin. Place it in a sieve/strainer and, using the fork again, break the pulp, pressing at the same time to remove all the water. Weigh the pulp, then weigh out half the amount of sugar.

Place the pulp in the saucepan again. Add the sugar (50% of the weight of the pulp), the lemon juice and lemon peel. Start stirring over a medium heat until all the sugar has dissolved. If needed add some of the reserved cooking water. It will start taking on a colour – a golden colour for the spaghetti squash or a transparent lighter colour for the cidra squash. Increase the heat and bring to the boil, stirring frequently, until it becomes the texture of jam/jelly.

Leave to cool down, then transfer to a sterilized jar. It can be stored in the fridge for 2 weeks.

Index

Acknowledgements

I am so grateful to my son Daniel Taylor, a great cook with whom I have shared thoughts and recipes while preparing this book. Two brilliant bakers, my daughter-in-law, Catherine and also her mother, my dear friend Brenda, have helped with the breads and the sweets chapter. With both I have often had the pleasure of sharing my kitchen in London and in Aracena. Another important name has to be added to this list, Madeleine Lee-Pearse. She came to my rescue when I had a broken hand and needed to test a number of recipes.

I could not end without expressing my sincere gratitude to a very unique publisher Ryland, Peters and Small. It has been a privilege to work with a competent, creative and helpful team of professionals while writing this book: Julia Charles Editorial Director; Abi Waters Senior Editor; Leslie Harrington Creative Director; Megan Smith Senior Designer; Photographers Nassima Rothacker & Clare Winfield; Food Stylist Kathy Kordalis; Prop Stylist Lauren Miller; Production Manager Gordana Simakovic and finally the brilliant illustrator Alex Green.

Picture credits

All photography by Nassima Rothacker except on the following pages:

Clare Winfield: pages 2–3; 47; 51; 52; 54; 91; 112–113; 115; 119; 120; 123; 124; 126; 135; 145; 146; 149; 150; 153.

Essay spreads: 14 left dbrnjhrj/Adobe Stock; 14 right RPS/Nassima Rothacker;15 left dbrnjhrj/Adobe Stock; 15 right Laiotz/Adobe Stock; 16–17 SeanParonePhoto/Adobe Stock; 44 above left julia.mlozano/Adobe Stock; 44 above right quasarphotos/Adobe Stock; 44 below quasarphotos/Adobe Stock; 45 above left idea_studio/Adobe Stock; 45 above right MCarmen/Adobe Stock; 45 below David/Adobe Stock; 60 left Lukasa Janyst/Adobe Stock; 60 right luisfpizarro/Adobe Stock; 61 above left etfoto/Adobe Stock; 61 above right Fernando/Adobe Stock; 61 below Oksana/Adobe Stock; 62–63 anetlanda/Adobe Stock; 94 left JMDuran Photography/Adobe Stock; 94 right AngelLuis/Adobe Stock; 95 left Dellealpi/Adobe Stock; 95 right Jose Muñoz Carrasco/Adobe Stock; 96–97 Roel/Adobe Stock; 130 left jarcosa/Adobe Stock; 130 right Edalin/Adobe Stock; 131 left Q77photo/Adobe Stock; 131 right diegogandi/Adobe Stock; 132–133 sphraner/Adobe Stock; 156 above left Sofia/Adobe Stock; 156 above right paolo Gallo/Adobe Stock; 156 below right Angelou/Adobe Stock; 157 left ahau1969/Adobe Stock; 157 right Nick Stubbs/Adobe Stock; 158–159 Uwe/Adobe Stock.

To David, my friend, my love

Senior Designer Megan Smith
Senior Editor Abi Waters
Production Manager
   Gordana Simakovic
Creative Director
   Leslie Harrington
Editorial Director Julia Charles

Illustrator Alex Green
Food Stylist Kathy Kordalis
Prop Stylist Lauren Miller
Indexer Hilary Bird

First published in 2024 by
Ryland Peters & Small
20–21 Jockey's Fields, London
WC1R 4BW
and
341 E 11th St
New York, NY 10029

10 9 8 7 6 5 4 3 2 1

ISBN: 978-1-78879-587-6

A CIP record for this book is available from the British Library. US Library of Congress cataloging-in-Publication Data has been applied for.

Notes

· All spoon measurements are level unless otherwise specified
5 ml = 1 teaspoon
15 ml = 1 tablespoon
· Uncooked or partially cooked eggs should not be served to the very old, frail, young children, pregnant women or those with compromised immune systems.
· When a recipe calls for the grated zest of citrus fruit, buy unwaxed fruit and wash well before using.
· Ovens should be preheated to the specified temperatures.
· To sterilize preserving jars, wash them in hot, soapy water and rinse in boiling water. Place in a large saucepan and cover with hot water. With the saucepan lid on, bring the water to the boil and continue boiling for 15 minutes. Turn off the heat and leave the jars in the hot water until just before they are to be filled. Invert the jars onto a clean dish towel to dry. Sterilize the lids for 5 minutes, by boiling (remove any rubber seals first). Jars should be filled and sealed while they are still hot.